Thinkback

A User's Guide to Minding the Mind

Thinkback

A User's Guide to Minding the Mind

Jack Lochhead
DeLiberate Thinking
Conway, Massachusetts

2001

LAWRENCE ERLBAUM ASSOCIATES, PUBLISHERS
Mahwah, New Jersey London

Lawrence Erlbaum Associates, Inc., Publishers
10 Industrial Avenue
Mahwah, NJ 07430

Cover design by Kathryn Houghtaling Lacey

Library of Congress Cataloging-in-Publication Data

Lochhead, Jack, 1944–
Thinkback : a user's guide to minding the mind / by Jack Lochhead.
p. cm.
Includes bibliographical references and index.
ISBN 0-8058-3342-0 (pbk. : alk. paper)
1. Problem solving—Problems, exercises, etc.
2. Comprehension—Problems, exercises, etc.
3. Reasoning—Problems, exercises, etc. I.. Title: Thinkback.
II. Title.
BF449 .L63 2000
153.4—dc21

00-024518
CIP

Books published by Lawrence Erlbaum Associates are printed on acid-free paper, and their bindings are chosen for strength and durability.

Printed in the United States of America
10 9 8 7 6 5 4 3 2 1

Contents

Foreword

No one knows what will be the result of a massive experiment currently underway in American education. Nearly every state has adopted new content standards, demanding that students master more complex subject matter than was formerly thought possible. Many of the standards specifically call for students to apply knowledge in ways that require abstract intelligence: They will analyze, compare, estimate, evaluate, and conclude. Advocates are confident that, with higher expectations and appropriate incentives, students will meet the challenge. Skeptics worry about too much too soon and doubt that negative incentives such as retention in grade will achieve their purpose. Meanwhile, teachers are on the spot, accountable not only for getting students to learn more but for producing better thinkers in the process.

This book can help. Jack Lochhead knows from long personal experience and from research that the simple but effective strategy described here can, in fact, improve students' intellectual skills. In spare, precise language, he explains why and how. The best way to sharpen any skill, he says, is practice with feedback. Because thinking is mostly invisible, we can get feedback on our thinking only if we somehow make it more visible. A good way to do that is to have thinkers talk out loud. And a practical way for them to get feedback on their thinking is by working in pairs, with one person thinking out loud and the other observing. Lochhead, who with Arthur Whimbey pioneered the use of this approach, calls it *Thinkback*.

Of course Thinkback is not quite as easy as it sounds. Is successful use, like that of any teaching strategy, depends on skillful implementation. But it is practical, not esoteric. It requires no special facilities or expensive equipment. And as Lochhead shows with his specific chapter-by-chapter examples, it can be used for a variety of purposes in different subject areas.

One of the most exciting revelations for many educators is the idea that not only can we help young people acquire knowledge and skills but we can actually enhance their mental abilities, giving them the capability to continue learning in the future. Educators intent on preparing their students to meet higher standards of academic performance now have a useful and powerful tool. Teach them Thinkback.

—Ron Brandt
Executive Editor Emeritus, Educational Leadership

Preface

WHO NEEDS TO READ THIS BOOK?

This book is for college and high school teachers who would like their students to be more intelligent and are willing to work to see that they become so. The book may also be useful to parents with similar concerns. For far too many years a powerful clique of psychologists has argued that it is impossible to increase intelligence because that ability is determined at birth. Fortunately, most of us have never fully believed these experts, because our own experience shows them to be wrong. In 1975, Arthur Whimbey published his first book, *Intelligence Can Be Taught* (Whimbey, 1975), in which he laid down the overwhelming scientific evidence that intelligence is not fixed at birth and that, with consistent effort, we can dramatically improve our capacities. A few years later, a second book *Problem Solving and Comprehension* (Whimbey & Lochhead, 1979–1999) provided specific techniques for improving thinking and analytical reasoning. Since then, thousands of students have used these techniques to increase test scores, win National Merit Scholarships, and gain admission to top-ranked professional schools.

WHAT IS *THINKBACK* ABOUT?

Thinkback moves beyond the range of skills covered in *Problem Solving and Comprehension* and shows how the Thinkback strategy can be used to improve performance in many diverse contexts. All major academic disciplines are considered: English, mathematics, science, social studies, history, and so on. In addition, different levels of understanding and engagement are introduced. Thinkback, a modification of the Thinking Aloud strategy described in *Problem Solving and Comprehension,* can be as useful in the mastery of basic facts and vocabulary as in contemplating complex relationships among abstract concepts. Six quite different learning strategies were selected to illustrate the range of contexts in which Thinkback can be incorporated. Because these strategies were deliberately selected to sample a diverse range of applications, each individual reader is likely to find some strategies much more appealing than others.

Thinkback spans the wide gap between unstructured constructivist style instruction and lock-step memorization drills. Using Thinkback can convert a teacher-centered rote mastery lesson into an intellectually challenging student-centered exploration, while at the same time maintaining specific content mastery objectives. Yet Thinkback can also be used to add subtle structure to an open-ended creative exercise allowing students of all levels to benefit, and insuring that no one is left floundering. Thinkback enables teachers to determine what content will be learned while, at the same time, acknowledging that only students are in full control of the learning process itself.

Thinkback is a tool for student empowerment. It is a strategy students can use to improve both their ability to think and their ability to learn. The Thinkback classroom, on the other hand, is a design for teacher liberation. In the Thinkback classroom teachers are able to see learning more clearly than they ever could before. Armed with this new observational tool, teachers can quickly discover powerful instructional strategies that make teaching more exciting and more effective.

HOW IS THE BOOK ORGANIZED?

This book is divided into eight chapters. Chapters 1 and 2 provide an introduction to the process and chapters 3 through 8 illustrate how the process can be used in various contexts. Thinkback is most effective when used in conjunction with other powerful tools for learning. The six application chapters are but a very small sampling of the combinations that can be constructed. The presentation of each topic is brief and intentionally incomplete. It is intended to serve as an invitation to further investigation rather than a detailed instruction manual. These chapters more closely resemble an illustrated travel brochure than a guide book or map. They will have accomplished their objective if they inspire you to explore the terrain and perhaps, eventually, to make your own map of it.

Chapter 1 introduces Thinkback with the sports metaphor of using instant replays to analyze success or failure. It shows how Thinkback provides video-like feedback in the domain of mental activity.

Chapter 2 describes how the Thinkback process works in the classroom. It suggests what teachers should and should not be doing during Thinkback-based instruction.

Chapter 3 explores the use of Thinkback as a tool for learning from graphic organizers. The materials are derived from the work of Barry Beyer and his text *Improving Student Thinking* with special attention to the role of scaffolding.

Chapter 4 uses examples from the Whimbey Writing Program to illustrate how Thinkback can be a tool for improving writing skills. In this chapter, the shaping paradigm is used to gradually improve performance, building from natural skills we all possess to the refined techniques of expert writers.

Chapter 5 explores problem solving using David Perkins' Knowledge as Design strategy to examine questions in history, political science, rhetoric and mathematics. This chapter returns to the scaffolding metaphor illustrating its application in relatively complex investigations.

Chapter 6 examines the role of memory in mathematics and understanding. It uses a strategy from John R. Hayes' book *The Complete Problem Solver* to illustrate how rote learning and understanding can profitably co-exist.

Chapter 7 explores the territory of concept mapping as described in Joseph Novak's *Learning, Creating and Using Knowledge*. The chapter lays out several different examples and concludes with an attempt to map the Thinkback strategy itself.

Chapter 8 examines Thinkback in an informal educational setting such as one might find at home. This chapter also provides a quick glimpse of Landamatics, an instructional strategy that can be used to view thinking skills at an even finer level of detail than that which can be attained through Thinkback by itself.

PART ONE

THE THINKBACK PROCESS: AN INTRODUCTION

CHAPTER ONE

Thinking With Thinkback

GETTING READY

Thinkback is a learning strategy that helps teachers and students view and better understand the mental processes used in thinking. Thinking is never easy and learning to use Thinkback requires both time and effort. A reasonable reader will want to know if it is worth the struggle. Let us review some of the evidence.

We begin with *Newsweek* reporter Ellis Cose's description of a program at Xavier University (Cose, 1997). Xavier is a small, historically Black university in New Orleans; there is a good chance that, until now, you have not heard of it. The Xavier program does not use Thinkback but rather its main ingredient, *Thinking Aloud Pair Problem Solving* (TAPPS).

> In the early 1970's, Xavier's record in training students for the sciences was solidly second-rate.... Only a handful of students, four or five a year, were making the leap to medical school.... Francis, who had been named president a few years earlier, decided things had to change. He turned to J. W. Carmichael, an energetic, young chemistry professor, and named him the premed adviser....
>
> Carmichael and his colleague attacked the problem with zeal, picking up information and teaching hints wherever they could find them. They tested a range of methods in the classroom, searching for the special combination of elements that would work. As Carmichael acknowledged, "We didn't start from some theoretical base." The theory, however, came quickly, thanks, in large measure, to Arthur Whimbey, a psychologist and testing expert whose book *Intelligence Can Be Taught* was published in 1975 and who shortly thereafter became involved with the Xavier effort.
>
> Whimbey's creed is summed up in his book's title. Intelligence ("skill at interpreting materials accurately and mentally reconstructing the relation-

> ships," as Whimbey defines it) can be taught much like skiing or playing the piano. By forcing students to think about every step in the problem-solving process and providing feedback as they go along, one can correct their bad reasoning habits, he insisted. One method is to pair students up and have one solve a mathematics problem aloud (a practice Whimbey calls "thinking-aloud problem solving") as the partner critiques the analysis....
>
> In 1977, the school [Xavier] launched a summer program called SOAR (for Stress on Analytical Reasoning). Aimed at students who had not yet started college, the program immediately became the foundation of Xavier's educational uplift efforts.... [T]he heart of the program is intense work: on reading skills, mathematics, vocabulary building, and exercises in abstract reasoning—many of which are from a book coauthored by Whimbey and J. Lochhead entitled *Problem Solving and Comprehension.*
>
> The approach seems to work. In 1993, forty-nine graduates of Xavier were accepted to medical schools, moving Xavier ahead of the significantly larger Howard University in the number of black graduates placed on the road to physicianhood. The following year, the number rose to fifty-five, and the year after that, to seventy-seven—putting Xavier far out front of any other university in America in the number of blacks placed in medical schools.... (The number has continued to rise ever since, it was 96 in 1998 and will be well over 100 in 1999!)
>
> Xavier's most impressive accomplishment, however, is not in the number of medical school slots it has won, but in its success in fostering an atmosphere of achievement ... the typical SOAR student gained about three grade levels on the Nelson-Denny Reading Test and the equivalent of 120 points on the Scholastic Aptitude Test (SAT). (Cose, 1997, pp. 55–57)[1]

The story Cose tells about Xavier is even more amazing than these short excerpts can convey. As measured by medical school slots won, Xavier's improvement has been more than 20 fold or 2,000%!! Yet, medical school acceptances are only a small part of the gains at Xavier. Many other majors have made similar gains. And the pace of improvement is even greater today than it was 10 years ago. For the latest details, search for SOAR at www.xula.edu.

The success of Xavier shows us what is possible. But it also shows us the level of effort required. Although an individual can raise reading and SAT scores in a month of hard work, an institution takes far longer to show progress. The Xavier story has unfolded over 20 years. It has been 20 years of superb leadership and strong faculty drive. Few schools have had the good fortune that would support such a sustained effort. Although the Whimbey program has been a key element of that success, it is only one of many key programs. Only the totality of all these programs creates the environment that makes the difference.

---

[1]Permission to reprint this extended quote from *Color-Blind* (Cose, 1997) was most graciously extended by HarperCollins Publishers, Inc.

Another success story is found in the Morningside Academy of Seattle Washington. For the past 20 years, the Academy has combined Thinking Aloud Problem Solving with a number of other techniques to produce substantial gains in both reading and mathematics as determined by such standardized measures as the Iowa Test of Basic Skills (ITBS). According to Michael Fabrizio, head teacher at Morningside, 3 months of instruction in TAPS followed by 5 months of math instruction produces substantial gains. In one case, students improved an average of 4 ITBS grade levels after only 5 months of mathematics instruction. Additional information is available at www.morningsideinfo.com. Other programs that use the Thinking Aloud Pair Problem Solving strategy can be found through the links section of www.whimbey.com.

While the Xavier and Morningside programs show what can be done, they also reflect the results of a long term commitment to comprehensive instructional change. Thinkback cannot instantly raise your students' scores. At best it will launch you on a journey toward that destination. The Thinkback strategy described in this book can significantly improve mental performance, but that improvement will not last if it is not sustained by an environment that encourages and rewards thinking and understanding. The need for such an environment is perhaps best described by the student who said "I know that you are trying to teach me to think. But that is not going to help me get through this university."

The issues involved in creating environments that encourage thinking extend far beyond the focus of this book, beyond even what can be covered in any single book. An excellent introduction to the subject can be found in *Understanding by Design* (Wiggins & McTighe, 1998). However, no book can ever substitute for the direct experience of struggling to make improved thinking the focus of your efforts.

THE THINKBACK KEY TO BETTER MANAGING THE MIND

Learning is often accomplished through imitation. Parents act; offspring imitate. This is how birds learn to fly, cats learn to hunt, and human children learn to walk and talk. However, thinking is very difficult to imitate because it is nearly impossible to "see" it happening. What we see are the results not the process. Imagine how hard it would be to learn to play a sport if the only part of the sport you could see was the score board. All the action would be invisible. You would have no idea of the number of players or of the rules. Occasionally, you might hear a cheer and see some numbers on the score board change. The chances are good that you would soon lose interest.

Thinkback is named after instant video *playback*, the process that has revolutionized sports. Players get immediate feedback on how they performed by watching their own actions from a perspective they could never achieve without the aid of a camera and video tape. They can be coached by an expert who can play back their actions in slow motion and demonstrate frame by frame where a motion was appropriate and where it was ineffective. Referees can replay their last call and rethink their last decision. Fans can watch the best (and worst) plays over and over, learning, gloating, and groaning.

Thinkback is also a generalization of techniques described in *Problem Solving and Comprehension,* a program with more than 20 years of success and research behind it. The key element of this program is TAPPS, a process that provides for thinkers and their minds what the video camera and tape player provide for athletes and their bodies.

Thinkback combines the method of TAPPS with the concept of making a *thought image* of the mind in action. In this book, we illustrate how the Thinkback technique can be used to develop any desired mental skill. The book provides only a quick survey, touching a few key points and leaving out many details. It is intended to develop an appreciation of the very wide range of potential applications to which Thinkback can be put and to inspire readers to investigate areas beyond those considered in the following few pages.

MOVING FORWARD WITH THINKBACK

Imagine you are at a dance. Suddenly the band starts playing an unfamiliar tune and everyone starts moving in ways you have never seen before. It is the new dance craze and you don't know a thing about it. What do you do? You watch. You try to figure out what people are doing and when they are doing it. Is there a specific sequence? Is there a core series of steps or motions you can start with before elaborating that pattern with fancier twists?

Now imagine you are in a math class. The teacher starts filling up the blackboard with numbers, letters, and funny signs. Chalk dust is flying in all directions. What do you do? If you are looking for patterns and sequences in the symbols written on the board, you are not likely to find any. The symbols on the board are a mere sketch of the thinking that goes on inside the head of the teacher. In all likelihood you cannot see or hear that thinking. It is invisible.

Thinking, unfortunately, is usually as invisible and silent as a stealth bomber viewed on an outdated radar screen.

Silent thinking, like a stealth aircraft, is virtually impossible to detect or shoot down. It streaks in, hits the target, and is gone. No one knows what has happened. This is very useful in warfare but not terribly productive in teaching. In teaching, we want thinking that is noisy, slow, and easy to detect. After the thinking has gone and the target has been hit, we want the observers to know what has happened and how it was done.

Thinking aloud is a slow, noisy process that makes thinking easy to see, easy to detect, and easy to shoot down. It is not the kind of thinking you would want to use in a debate (or on a test), but it is the kind of thinking we ought to find in classrooms and other learning situations. Thinking aloud allows for learning by imitation and it allows coaching to improve performance.

Here are two examples of thinking aloud taken from *Problem Solving and Comprehension* (Whimbey & Lochhead, 1979, 1999). Before the thinking is shown, the original problem is stated and, after that, the problem solver's solution is given.

Original Problem

If the circle below is taller than the square and the cross is shorter than the square, put a *K* in the circle. However, if this is not the case, put a *T* in the second tallest figure.

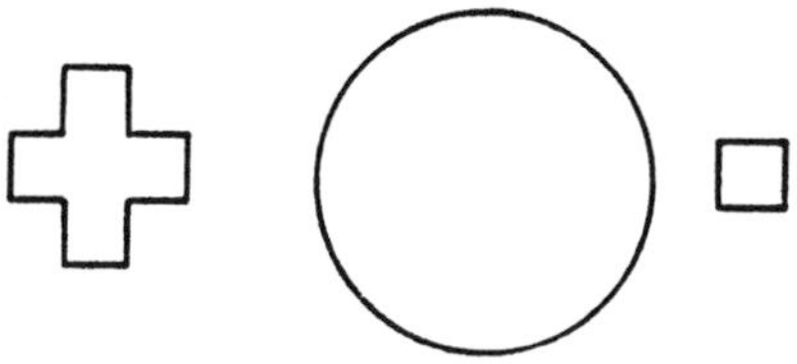

Problem Solver's Response[2]

Note. Read both the comments on the left and the problem solver's report on the right. Quotation marks show when the problem solver read aloud. The absence of quotation marks indicates that the problem solver was thinking aloud.

The Problem Solver read and thought aloud.

"If the circle below is taller than the square and the cross is shorter than the square, put a *K* in the circle."

Let me start again.

"If the circle below" ... I'll put my finger on the circle ... "is taller than the square." ... Yes, the circle is taller than the square.

"And the cross is shorter than the square" ... I'll move my finger from the cross to the square and compare them ... this part is false ... the cross is not shorter than the square.

"Put a *K* in the circle."

[2] The problem solver is an outstanding medical student who earned a Master's degree in Comparative Literature before deciding to enter the field of medicine.

So I shouldn't put a *K* in the circle. Part of the statement is false. I would only write *K* if both the first part and the second part were true.

I should read the whole sentence again and see if my conclusion is correct.

"If the circle is taller than the square" ... Yes ... "and the cross is shorter than the square" ... No.... "Put a *K* in the circle" ... I didn't. That's correct.

As the Problem Solver reread the sentence, she moved her finger first from the circle to the square and then from the cross to the square.

I'll continue to the next part of the problem.

"However, if this is not the case" ... and it isn't the case ... "put a *T* in the second tallest figure."

The second tallest figure is the cross so I'll put a *T* in the cross.

Another Example

Here is the response that an experienced problem solver (a lawyer) gave to another problem. Note how carefully he checks everything, and even stops for a moment in deciding right from left.

Original Problem

> If the word *sentence* contains less than 9 letters and more than 3 vowels, circle the first vowel. Otherwise circle the consonant which is farthest to the right in the word.

Problem Solver's Response

The Problem Solver read the entire problem aloud.

"If the word *sentence* contains less than 9 letters and more than 3 vowels, circle the first vowel. Otherwise circle the consonant which is farthest to the right in the word."

I'll start from the beginning.

"If the word *sentence* contains less than 9 letters."

The Problem Solver pointed to the letters with his pen as he counted.

I'll count the letters in *sentence*. *1, 2, 3, 4, 5, 6, 7, 8*. Let me check it. *1, 2, 3, 4, 5, 6, 7, 8*. So it does have less than 9 letters. I'll write the word *yes* above the problem. That way I'll remember it.

The Problem Solver wrote yes over the sentence (see original problem).

The Problem Solver resumed reading.

"And more than 3 vowels."

The Problem Solver pointed with his pen as he counted.

1, 2, 3. Let me check that. *1, 2, 3*. It contains exactly 3 vowels, not more than 3 vowels. I'll write *no* on the problem to remind me.

"Circle the first vowel."

So I won't do that.

"Otherwise circle the consonant which is farthest to the right in the word."

The consonant farthest to the right? Let me see. Which is my right hand? This is my right hand. OK, so the last letter is the one farthest to the right. But the last letter is *E*. The next letter over is *C*. So it is the consonant farthest to the right. I'll circle the *C*.

These examples were selected to illustrate how clear and accurate thinking aloud can be. But thinking aloud is not always so perfect.

In one of the great classic studies of thinking, *Problem Solving Processes of College Students*, Bloom and Broder (1950) reported on students who were inexperienced in thinking aloud. They provide six student solutions to the following problem.

Figure Analogies

In each line below, find the rule by which Figure A is changed to make Figure B. Apply the rule to Figure C. Select the resulting figure at the right and blacken the corresponding answer space.

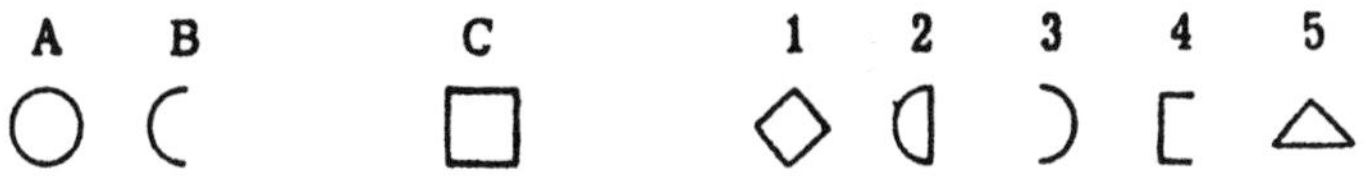

Student Solutions

John J: "One-half circle, so one-half square—Number 4."

Edward F: "Figure A is halved to make B, so Figure C is halved to make number 4."

Dorothy S: "A to B—merely cut A. C to 1—turn C to equal 1. I think that's the nearest—no, cut C equals 4."

Betty K: "Oh, they're taking away half of it, so the answer would be 4."

Thomas N: "I have an idea of something which is the left half of a whole—seeing this is a square, be looking for the left half of a square and find 4 right away."

George R: "Geometrical, I guess. Circle and one-half of a circle cut off to the left. Square and one-half of a square cut off to the left. I choose 4." (Bloom & Broder, 1950, p. 2)

Bloom and Broder (1950) also reported on students who found the task of thinking aloud to be virtually impossible.

> A few students were almost entirely unable to reveal the processes they employed in the attack on problems. They read the problem, gave the answer almost immediately, but were unable to explain or reveal how they had arrived at such a solution. If pressed, they made up a suitable explanation, but it was evident that the entire process had taken place a little too quickly for them to observe it or to be conscious of it. (p. 23)

If thinking aloud is to be a useful tool in instruction, and this entire book is based on that assumption, then something must be done to help students (and teachers) learn to master it.

TAPPS is a technique that was invented by Whimbey in the 1970s and has since been refined and expanded by thousands of teachers and their students. It is designed to add a self-improvement feedback loop to the thinking-aloud process so that no matter how tentative one's initial efforts, practice (and conscious attention to detail) will make perfect. Here is an example from *Problem Solving and Comprehension* (1979, 1999):

Problem

If the second letter of the word *west* comes after the fourth letter in the alphabet, circle the letter A below. If it does not, circle the B.

A B

	Problem Solver
The Problem Solver reads the problem.	" 'If the second letter in the word *west* comes after the fourth letter in alphabet, circle the letter A below. If it does not, circle the B.' "
	Listener
	"You said 'in alphabet' not 'in *the* alphabet.' "

Problem Solver

"Oh yeah." (Pause)

Listener

"What are you thinking?"

Problem Solver

"Nothing. I am just looking at it." (Pause)

Listener

"What are you looking at?"

Problem Solver

"It's A. I circle the A."

Listener

"Wait a minute. You just said you weren't thinking. Now you say it's A. How did you get that?"

Problem Solver

"Well, the fourth letter is *d*."

Listener

"Yes."

Problem Solver

"And so I circle the A."

Listener

"How do you get the fourth letter is *d*?"

Problem Solver

"A, B, C, D. I count."

Listener

"OK. So how come you circle A?"

Problem Solver

"Because that's what it says to do."

Listener

"I think you are wrong."

Here the Listener lies deliberately.

Problem Solver

"I am wrong?" (Pause) "You mean it's B. It can't be B because the letter *e* comes after the letter *d*."

Listener

"Yeah?"

Problem Solver

"And it says that if the second letter in west, which is *e*, comes after the fourth letter in the alphabet circle the A. So I did."

Listener

The Listener tests the Problem Solver's confidence by trying another interpretation.

"Yes, but e comes before h, which is the fourth letter in alphabet."

Problem Solver

"Hmm. You think they want the fourth letter in *alphabet*? (Pause) No they don't, they said *the* alphabet not in alphabet. You pointed that out to me earlier."

Listener

"Oh."

Problem Solver

"So it's A."

Listener

"Wait, tell me all over why you think it is A—go slowly."

Problem Solver

"Well the problem asks you to circle the A if the second letter in *west* which is e comes after the fourth letter in the alphabet which is *d*. And *e* does come after *d* so I circle the A."

Listener

"Are you sure?

Problem Solver

"Yes."

In this example the Listener never gets the Problem Solver to talk in adequate detail, but through a variety of techniques does get the Problem Solver to talk some.

However, although the addition of a listener provides the thinking-aloud problem solver with valuable guidance and feedback, the listener's role is itself far from easy to learn. Fortunately, even a poor listener gives valuable help to a thinker who is struggling to make thinking audible. As the listener and problem solver practice their respective roles, they inevitably improve each other's efforts.

Because the role of the listener is absolutely key both to making thinking audible and to the self-correcting aspect of TAPPS, *Problem Solving and Comprehension* describes the listener's role at some length. It even includes an extended verbatim transcript (including the errors of real speech) generated by a pair of graduate students skilled in the roles of problem solver and listener.

Role of the Listener When Working With a Partner

As noted earlier, if you are using this book in a class your teacher may ask you to work in pairs. One partner should read and think aloud, while the other partner listens. On subsequent problems the partners should change roles, taking turns as problem solver and listener.

The partner who listens plays an important role in the learning process. He should not sit back inattentively with his mind elsewhere. Instead, he should concentrate on two functions. He should: *1.* continually check accuracy, and *2.* demand constant vocalization.

1. *Continually Check Accuracy*

Since accuracy is all-important, the listener should continually check the accuracy of the problem solver. This includes every computation he makes, every diagram he draws, every conclusion he reaches. In other words, the problem solver's accuracy should be checked at every step of the problem, not just when he gives his final answer. For example, if in working the problem shown earlier the problem solver concluded that the word *sentence* has nine letters, the listener should have immediately caught the error and pointed it out.

Catching errors involves several activities. First, the listener must actively work along with the problem solver. He should follow every step the problem solver takes, and he should be sure he understands each step. If the listener takes a passive attitude—if he does not actively think through each step—he won't know for sure whether or not the problem solver's steps are totally correct.

Second, the listener should never let the problem solver get ahead of him. This may often mean that the listener will have to ask the problem solver to wait a moment so that he can check a conclusion. In this program the emphasis is on accuracy, not on speed. Both the problem solver and the listener should concentrate on accuracy. If the listener needs a moment to verify a conclusion, this will give the problem solver a chance to go over his work and check his own thinking. The problem solver should, in the back of his mind, constantly have the thought "Is that correct—should I check that?" as he works a problem. This will slow him down a little so that the listener will be able to keep pace. However, if the problem solver is working too hastily, at the expense of accuracy, the listener should ask him to slow down—so that he can follow accurately and analytically. Moreover, even if the problem solver is not working too hastily to be accurate, the listener may still occasionally ask him to stop a moment while he checks a point he is unsure of.

Third, the listener should not work the problem separately from the problem solver. When some listeners first learn the procedure used in this program, they turn away from the problem solver and work the problem completely on their own. Occasionally they even finish the problem long before the problem solver. This is incorrect. The listener should listen. He should actively work along with the problem solver, not independently of him.

Finally, when the listener catches an error he should only point it out—**he should never give the correct answer**. By the same token, if the listener sees an answer or a conclusion before the problem solver sees it, he should not furnish it, but should wait for the problem solver to work it out. If the problem solver seems completely stuck, the listener may provide a suggestion on the first step to take. But he should not actually take the first step and obtain a partial answer. Instead, the problem solver should do all the work.

In summary, the listener should understand that he is not being picky or overly critical of his partner when he points out errors. He is helping him improve his scholastic problem solving skill—a skill that will be useful in all academic courses. The listener should check every step taken and every conclusion reached by the problem solver. He should never let the problem solver go on to a second step until he checks the first one. And when he detects an error he should point it out without actually correcting it.

2. *Demand Constant Vocalization*

The second function of the listener is to insure that the problem solver vocalizes all of the major steps he takes in solving a problem. Thinking aloud is a primary part of this program. It is the only way to communicate and to monitor thinking. It should not be neglected. Even the solution of simple problems should be vocalized entirely—so that vocalizing can be done easily when difficult problems are met. If the problem solver skips through one or more steps without thinking aloud, the listener should ask him to explain his thoughts at that point.

An Example

The roles of the problem solver and listener are demonstrated in the following dialogue between two graduate students working a problem. As you read through the example, notice how the listener helps the problem solver both to be more accurate and to keep talking. The listener is always following what the problem solver is saying and at the same time looking for ways to make the problem solver think harder about the problem.

Problem Solver

The Problem Solver begins by reading the problem twice.

" 'Bill, Judy and Sally have the occupations of teacher, plumber and teamster but not necessarily in that order. Bill is shorter than Judy but taller than Sally. The plumber is the tallest and the teamster is the shortest. What is Judy's occupation?' Now you want to see how to solve that? OK. Let's see. I would read it again. 'Bill, Judy and Sally have the occupations of teacher, plumber and teamster but not necessarily in that order. Bill is shorter than Judy but taller than Sally. The plumber is the tallest and the teamster is the shortest. What is Judy's occupation?' So I would go back to where it says Bill is shorter than Judy but taller than Sally and I would note that in some way. Um, I guess using lines to indicate, you know, some kind of length.

Sally < Bill < Judy

No I wouldn't. I would just write their names down in the order that it gives. So I'd have Bill is less than Judy but taller than Sally—common inequality."

Listener

Here the Listener probably understands the Problem Solver's notation but is looking for a more detailed explanation. It is always a good idea to ask the Problem Solver to explain any new symbol.

"OK. So you're using inequality signs here?"

Problem Solver

teamster_plumber

"Yeah. Just to show and er, well they indicate height; unequal height. So it could be read the height of Bill is less than the height of Judy and greater than the height of Sally. Then it says the plumber is the tallest of these three so I would write down the word plumber and the teamster is the shortest. And so I where I'd put whatever occupation er, in the middle indicating that the person who is occupied in that manner has the middle height. And then to the left of that I'm going to write teamster."

The Listener is trying to get the Problem Solver to explain the diagram in more detail.

Listener

"Ok. So first you wrote plumber and you put that on the right-hand side?"

Problem Solver

"Right. And then I left a space for some other occupation and then I wrote teamster on the left-hand side, indicating that the teamster is the shortest and the plumber is the tallest."

Note that while this may seem like a silly question it does get the Problem Solver to reflect more carefully on the problem. In particular, it forces an explicit statement of the implied connection between the two diagrams.

Listener

"Why do you put the plumber on the right-hand side? Any reason for that?"

Problem Solver

"No, I could have just as easily put the plumber on the left-hand side except that above it I have the inequality going from right to left meaning that Judy who is the tallest and then Bill who is the next tallest, and then Sally who is the next tallest. So that's probably why I have plumber who is the tallest on the right-hand side under Judy, and teamster who is the shortest on the left-hand side under Sally."

Listener

"Do you think that's why you put it there?"

Problem Solver

"Yeah, I think that's why I put it there. Because I had set the precedent with Sally, less than Bill, less than Judy, going from left to right.

"Uh, so the final question is what is Judy's occupation, and I think that Judy is the plumber." (Pause)

Listener

Whenever the Problem Solver is quiet for more than a few seconds the Listener should ask for verbalization.

"What are you thinking now?"

Problem Solver

"That Judy is the plumber. That Judy is the plumber and I'm going to write um, teacher in between teamster and plumber."

Listener

Even though the Problem Solver seems to have solved the problem, the Listener keeps asking questions to make sure the problem is fully understood.

"Why?"

Problem Solver

teamster, teacher, plumber

"Because I think that uh, the teacher is of medium height. But I'm not sure so I'm going to go and check everything now.

Bill, Judy and Sally have the occupations of teacher, plumber and teamster but not necessarily in that order, meaning that Bill's not the teacher and Judy's not the plumber and Sally's not the teamster."

Here the Listener notices that the Problem Solver's words suggest confusion between the terms "not necessarily" and "not." A simple question prompts the Problem Solver to be more careful.

Listener

"It means that they're not that?"

Problem Solver

"It says 'but not necessarily in that order,' yeah so Bill does not have to be the teacher. I think when you say 'that order' you mean respectively. You're saying not necessarily respectively. So Bill is not necessarily the teacher."

Listener

"Uh-huh."

Problem Solver

"Judy's not necessarily the plumber and Sally's not necessarily the teamster but it could be that way." (Pause)

Here again the Listener prompts the Problem Solver to keep talking.

Listener

"So what are you thinking now?"

Problem Solver

"So I was thinking that this inequality that I have written down is correct because it says that Bill is shorter than Judy and taller than Sally. So if Bill is shorter than Judy and taller than Sally, then Judy must also be taller than Sally because Bill is shorter than Judy, and Bill is taller than Sally. So if Judy is taller than Bill then she must be taller than Sally. So I'm fine with that particular statement. The plumber is the tallest and the teamster is the shortest. And since Judy is taller than Bill, and Bill is taller than Sally and then Judy is taller than Sally so Judy is the tallest and the plumber is the tallest and so Judy is the plumber. And the teamster is the shortest and since Sally is let's see—(mumbles to self)—So Judy is shorter than Bill and Judy is shorter than Sally and the teamster is the shortest so I think that Judy is the teamster."

The Listener tries to see if the Problem Solver notices that this contradicts the earlier statement.

Listener

"So you just said Judy is the teamster."

Problem Solver

"Right. What did I say before, then, she was the plumber?"

Listener

"Uh-huh."

Problem Solver

"Did I say that?"

Listener

"Yeah."

Problem Solver

"And the teamster is the shortest. No, Sally's the teamster."

Listener

"So what were you just looking at?"

Problem Solver

"Just, you know, momentary dyslexia. Yeah. I'm going to say that Sally's the teamster, and Bill's the teacher and Judy's the plumber."

The Listener should always check to be sure the Problem Solver is confident before the pair move on to the next problem.

Listener

"Are you sure?"

Problem Solving and Comprehension also provides detailed instructions for the problem solver. We have not repeated them here because the instructions in *Problem Solving and Comprehension* are designed specifically for students who are struggling to master basic analytical thinking strategies. Instructions for the problem solver need to be tailored to both the skill level of the problem solver and to the context of the problems being solved. But one instruction is essential in all contexts. The problem solver must strive to *avoid stealth thinking*. That is, the problem solver must make a constant effort to describe his or her thinking as it happens and in as much detail as possible. This is not easy and it is often uncomfortable. This discomfort is most easily handled by keeping the goals of Thinkback clearly in mind. Thinkback is the use of the TAPPS strategy with the added vision of video playback. In Thinkback we use TAPPS to make a full-action movie of the mind at work—a *thought image*. Just as the video camera can capture the athlete's performance in minute detail, the thinking aloud strategy captures (for an instant) the thinker's thinking. If students keep in mind that the purpose of Thinkback is to capture the mind at work, and if they understand the video tape analogy to sports, then they are less likely to find the Thinkback strategy awkward.

A camcorder in unskillful hands creates the kind of home video that makes you dizzy and sick. With Thinkback, there is no camera operator to blame. Producing an accurate recording of the mind requires careful collaboration between the listener and the problem solver. Both partners play critical roles. When students have difficulty learning how to apply the TAPPS strategy of Thinkback it is usually because they are not focused on the goal of making a recording of the thinking process. They may be concerned about how slowly they are working. Thinkback is designed to slow down thinking so we can see it. They may be embarrassed that their approach to the problem lacks elegance. Thinkback is designed to reveal thinking so that we can study and improve it. Students may be frustrated by the extra effort required. Thinkback actually makes problems harder to solve. It forces us to go beyond the superficial solution to reach a far deeper understanding than is normally obtained.

A closer examination of the videotape analogy to sports reveals several crucial aspects of Thinkback. Although video tape can capture nearly all of the important motions made by an athlete it cannot show the level of determination, self-confidence, and enthusiasm that went into the performance. Similarly, a Thinkback recording captures certain aspects of thinking better than others. Some thinking is highly verbal and translates easily into the Thinkback medium. Other thinking is visual and thus converts much less easily and only after significant alteration. The process of trying to describe in words thinking that occurs in mental pictures, is a major intrusion into, and distortion of, the mental process. Although the athlete who performs before a camera is free to act normally, the thinker who thinks within Thinkback is giving a highly constrained performance. The "picture" that emerges is mostly recorded in words (although sketches on paper should also be used). Thus, the Thinkback recording is rather like an x-ray or a sonogram used to make images of our internal organs. The images are incomplete and require a great deal of interpretation to be read and understood.

As a listener and problem-solver pair become more practiced in their respective roles, they learn to make clearer pictures. The problem solver learns to think in a manner that is more easily put into words and sketches. The listener learns to better interpret the words and pictures, filling in missing data to generate a more complete image of the thinker's thinking. All of this changes thinking from what it would have been without the intrusion of Thinkback. Thus, one must ask, are these changes for the better? After 20 years of research, it is easy to answer in the affirmative, but this was not so obvious when the process was first introduced.

We now know that although Thinkback creates a new kind of thinking, it does not damage or destroy other modes of thinking. Outside of the Thinkback classroom, students remain free to use whatever kind of thinking they find most applicable. But with the addition of Thinkback to their modes of operation, they are now in a position to think, when appropriate, in a manner where the steps they make are clear and obvious. Visual thinkers can slow down the pictures that flash through their minds and describe important details. This is essential, first for detecting errors in reasoning and second, for convincing others of the logic of a correct argument.

The first skill, detecting errors in reasoning, is essential to any form of critical analysis. As the pace of technological change increases, more and more of what we do is based on reasoning from past experience rather than a simple replication of past routines. In these circumstances, the ability to detect errors in reasoning before they create a disaster can be a matter of life or death and, at the very least, can make or break a career. The second skill, the ability to convince others of the logic of an argument, has become increasingly important in the workplace as local job site teams replace corporate hierarchies. Today, workers at all levels are expected to reason on their own and to convince others of the logic behind their conclusions.

THINKBACK

Thinkbak is TAPPS used in conjunction with the vision of video playback and the notion of recording a *thought image*.

Thinkback = TAPPS + *Thought Image*

In Thinkback:

The *Problem Solver* strives to avoid stealth thinking.

The *Listener* tries to determine how the problem solver is thinking.

SUMMARY

In summary, Thinkback is designed to improve thinking by exposing normally hidden parts of the process. To keep this goal clearly in mind, we employ an analogy to the videotaping of athletic performances. However, because the "pictures" we "record" are less complete and less permanent than those recorded on videotape, it may be preferable to refer to them as "*thought images*" rather than recordings or pictures. Although the vast majority of students find Thinkback easy and natural to learn, a few find it awkward in the beginning. Twenty years of testing and evaluation have shown that the process is safe and effective for all students and that those who struggle with it at the beginning should simply be encouraged to persevere.

CHAPTER TWO

Teaching With Thinkback

EDUCATIONAL ERRORS

Thinking aloud is a slow, noisy process that makes thinking easy to see, easy to detect and easy to shoot down. But do we want thinking that can be shot down? One might think that we want only good examples, examples students can imitate and learn from. Many teachers worry that bad examples will only confuse students. If this is how you feel, you will not be happy with this book. We believe that bad examples are as critical to serious learning as are good examples. Learning from good examples may help you get to your goal quickly, but an experience that contains nothing but good examples cannot prepare you for those times when you are lost. Flawless exemplars cannot teach how to escape a bad situation. Thinking is not a simple, straightforward process that can be learned in one uniquely correct manner. Thinking is always a matter of balancing alternatives and selecting between options with incomplete information. Thinking involves going beyond the tried and proven paths to investigate possibilities that may go where no mind has ever gone before.

Imagine you are about to fly across the Atlantic ocean. You have a choice between two pilots. One pilot has never made a serious mistake or been in a dangerous situation; she has learned by imitating all the moves of a practiced senior instructor. The second pilot also has a perfect flight record, but in addition she has spent hours in a flight simulator where she has been placed in impossible situations in which a crash was unavoidable. In the simulator she has flown with one engine, pulled out of a powered dive, and extinguished a major engine fire. She has crash landed a badly damaged aircraft more than 100 times and survived nearly half of these simulated landings. Which pilot would you select?

Pilots and thinkers both need to experience failure to learn how to safely cope with difficult situations. Learning how to detect an erroneous argument is every bit as important as learning to appreciate a well-made proof. Furthermore, erroneous arguments often contain the seeds of brilliant new insights. Suppose I say it is noon now in New York, so it must be noon in Tokyo. This idea is false. It is never the same time in Tokyo as in New York. However, if it is not the same time everywhere at the same time, how come? How can it be a different time in New York than in Tokyo? Why did we design a time system that would be 25[1] different times all at the same time? Why couldn't we have designed a system that would be the same everywhere at once? It is only *after* considering all these different correct and incorrect possibilities that one begins to understand our global system of clocks. Considering only the right answers will never get you there.

TEMPERING TALK

There is a great deal in Thinkback that runs counter to common practice. In chapter 1, we considered the need to make thinking noisy so that we could see it. We have just considered ways in which examples of bad thinking help students better understand good thinking. Now we move on to consider why teachers ought to talk as little as possible.[2]

There are many things you can learn to do simply by being told how. You can learn how to turn on a computer by being told where the on/off switch is. You can learn what to read for homework by being told the name of the book and the page numbers. However, you cannot learn to touch-type on the computer keyboard or to read the material in the homework chapter simply by being told how. Nor can you learn these skills only by watching a skilled performer type or read. Complex skills can only be learned with the aid of hours and hours of active practice. Verbal instruction can guide and streamline the practice, but it cannot replace it. Usually a few words of instruction at the right time will be far more valuable than many hours of detailed instruction at the wrong time.

Efficient learning requires an appropriate balance between verbal instruction and practice, with, in most cases, the bulk of the time going to practice. But not all practice is equally effective. Closely monitored practice can be two to ten times as effective as unmonitored practice because faulty moves can be detected and corrected before they become bad habits.

Verbal instruction, whether in the form of words said by a teacher in a classroom or those written by an author in a text book, always competes with practice. One minute of classroom verbal instruction can prevent an hour or more of practice! Yes, one *hour* may be lost for every *minute* of verbalized teaching! This is be-

---

[1]This is not an error; the extra time is in India.

[2]In my own thinking about the teacher's role, I have been profoundly influenced by Radical Constructivism as elucidated by Ernst von Glasersfeld. However, the same conclusions can be reached from quite different assumptions.

cause it is not just one student who is being held back from practice, it is every student. (And if that practice were to take place in the Pair Problem Solving format suggested in this book, it would be at least doubly useful.) Thus, a class of 30 students can lose the equivalent of 60 minutes of practice during just one minute of verbal instruction.[3]

(The odds are even worse for an author. Thousands of people may be reading the words on this page and everyone of them will *not* be doing something else useful and important while they read these words. Every extra page could cost thousands of hours of practice, perhaps even important practice by that same pilot who will be flying planeloads of people across the Atlantic.)

The art of teaching, whether in the classroom or through a text book, is, in part, the art of keeping your mouth shut (or your keyboard still). In the classroom, the skilled teacher waits and watches until that precise moment where a few words will make a difference. *However, waiting will do no good if students are not engaged in the kind of activity that creates those moments in which verbal instruction can guide.* Thus, the skilled teacher also must structure activities that combine practice and challenge, opening up opportunities to learn. Thinkback is one such activity.

Finding those key moments when verbal instruction is useful and powerful is very difficult, even for those skilled teachers who know how to create the opportunities and recognize the openings. For one thing, such moments happen at different times for different students, and it is impossible for one teacher to be everywhere at once. However, it is not impossible for every student to have a partner, and there is nothing that says critical instruction must come from the teacher. Often, as I have wandered around my classroom listening to student conversations during Pair Problem Solving or some other form of cooperative learning, I found myself about to pounce with my precious moment of wise instruction when I realized that the students are articulating the idea themselves, sometimes far better than I could.

SHARING RESPONSIBILITY

Thinking Aloud Pair Problem Solving can be at least twice as valuable as an equal amount of time spent on individual practice because it provides students constant opportunities to learn from each other. However, these opportunities may be lost if either the teacher or the students believe that important instruction can

---

[3]One could argue that the 1 minute of verbal instruction should be counted as 30 minutes of learning as 30 students are listening to it. In practice, however, it is very rare that all students are listening and even rarer that more than one or two are in a position to benefit from what they hear. Thus, in only the best of circumstances is verbal instruction reaching most of its target. Practice, on the other hand, reaches everyone involved, although with differing degrees of impact.

only come directly from the teacher. Unfortunately, this belief is all too common. Ever since the decline of the one-room school house, our educational system has discouraged student–student instruction and instead placed a Sisyphusian instructional burden on the classroom teacher.

In the Thinkback classroom, both the teacher and the students need to accept that the majority of the instruction will be delivered by the students. Teacher and students must share a common faith that although errors will be made, these errors will, in due course, be corrected. All participants must understand that the detours and deviations introduced by student–student coaching have important value and create a more comprehensive map of the terrain being studied. The student dialogues presented in the following chapters illustrate how this system works and should convince the reader that learning in the Thinkback classroom is not governed by fluke and happenstance.

Although the Thinkback teacher may be freed from endlessly rolling the verbal instructional boulder, the tasks remaining are no less demanding. There is the need to keep tabs on the activity in the entire class to insure that students remain on task, to check that the materials being worked on are appropriate (neither too difficult nor too easy) and to guard against those rare occasions when the self-correcting features of Thinkback fail, and major misconceptions get propagated rather than weeded out. Most often, such misconceptions occur within one pair of students and may be challenged (and corrected) simply by having that pair discuss their work with a second pair who have solved things differently.

STOP, LOOK, AND LISTEN

The most important role for the teacher of a Thinkback classroom is to listen and learn. If the teacher sits quietly with a pair of students listening attentively to what they are saying, this conveys to the students that what they are engaged in is important. The teacher should do this, not with an eye to finding the first opportunity to interrupt with some words of wisdom, but rather with a serious interest in learning just how the students *are* thinking about the matter at hand. Are the students motivated to learn the material? Do they see in it some relevance to their lives? How well have they mastered the techniques of Thinking Aloud Pair Problem Solving? What is their understanding of the content under study? How well does the selected material challenge and expand the students' understanding of this content? The better the teacher understands the answers to these questions, the better the teacher becomes at his profession. And the better the teacher becomes, the less verbalizing the teacher needs to do and the more time the students have to practice and learn. Thinkback is above all else an opportunity for teachers to learn about learning.

Listening may be the teacher's first and most important activity, but it is far from the only one. Careful listening will reveal those important teachable moments where a few select words can guide students to major leaps in learning and understanding. Sometimes the teacher should utter these words, but more often the teacher can simply facilitate their utterance by bringing together a pair of students who have just solved a problem with a pair who are still struggling with it. This, of course, can only be done if the teacher is monitoring the activity in several different Thinkback pairs. Listening carefully to one pair while monitoring the activity among several is no small challenge.

BACK TO BASICS

So far this chapter has stressed the need for teachers to listen and for as much instruction as possible to flow out of student–student interactions rather than teacher–student directives. However, this does not mean that teachers never should lecture or that teachers should avoid all attempts to explain ideas and procedures. The art of teaching is in finding the right balance of these and other activities.

Earlier we mentioned that it can be useful to bring two pairs of students together so that one pair can help the other. There are times however, when such a strategy can backfire, and a misconception from one group may spread to the second. At these times it may be valuable to bring the entire class together and deliver a short lecture, keeping in mind that each minute costs 1 hour and that any misconception that spreads easily is not likely to be swept away by mere words. When such conceptual difficulties are revealed, it is a good idea to pay careful attention to how students are thinking about the concept and to continue to do this for days and weeks afterwards. It is essential to return frequently to the topic to re-examine how students are dealing with it. Often, misconceptions will be swept away only to re-appear once again as though they had never been dealt with in the first place (or the second, or third, etc.).

Thinkback can be an excellent preparation for lecture. In the later chapters of this book, there are several student dialogs in which students raise topics that could easily become the basis of one or more lectures. By placing a lecture *after* students have already introduced themselves to the topic, a certain degree of interest and involvement is assured. Furthermore, if the teacher has already been listening to student discussions of the topic, it is far easier to keep the lecture relevant and appropriate to the audience.

Much more could be said about teaching with Thinkback. How often should it be used? What kind of grading system is most useful? What is the best arrangement for the furniture? All these questions deserve attention and yet viable answers are as varied as effective teaching styles. In the spirit of keeping the monologues short and the time for practice high, we will now move on to the examples. These examples contain many important points about the Thinkback process itself and about teaching with Thinkback. Some of these points will be summarized at the end of the dialogue but many will not. This means that *you must read the dialogues* carefully if you are to benefit from what this book has to offer. The lessons you draw for yourself will be the ones that are most valuable to you. Nothing that we assemble for you will ever match the power of your own constructions.

PART TWO

USING THINKBACK IN DIVERSE CONTEXTS: ILLUSTRATIVE EXAMPLES

CHAPTER THREE

Grappling With Graphic Organizers

THE SCAFFOLD

When video recordings are used to improve the performance of athletes, the camera is focused on significant activities. Video recordings of athletes just "hanging out" usually have very little value for improving performance. For the Thinkback strategy to work, students must be engaged in a meaningful activity that challenges their minds. In the remaining chapters of this book we examine several such activities. We begin with one taken from *Improving Student Thinking* (Beyer, 1997).[1]

Beyer introduces Graphic Organizers within a chapter on Scaffolding. Scaffolding is a key concept not only for graphic organizers but for all of Thinkback. Here is how Beyer describes scaffolding:

> Scaffolding thinking consists of supporting student application of a cognitive operation by structuring the execution of that operation with verbal and/or visual prompts. Like a scaffold that holds up and gives form to a building under construction or a renovation, a thinking scaffold is a temporary, adjustable, skeletal structure that gives shape to a cognitive procedure in the process of its execution. It is a device or technique that frames a procedure in such a way that when it—the scaffold—is removed (as it eventually is), the procedure when executed retains the structure shaped by the scaffold. Students just beginning to apply a newly encountered or complex cognitive operation benefit immensely from having their initial attempts to practice that procedure scaffolded until they have internalized the procedure and can execute it on their own without external support.

---

[1]Quotes and Graphic Organizers reproduced from Beyer (1997). Beyer, *Improving Student Thinking: A Comprehensive Approach*. Copyright © 1997 by Barry K. Beyer (published by Allyn & Bacon). Reprinted by permission.

> Instructional techniques or devices that prove most useful as scaffolds for thinking possess two major characteristics. First, they frame or sequence the major steps in a procedure for carrying out the cognitive operation or skill they represent. A scaffold for problem solving, in effect, moves students through the steps in solving a problem. A scaffold for detecting bias moves students, step by step, through a cognitive procedure for carrying out this operation. Second, these devices are used by students *while they are engaged* in executing the cognitive operation being scaffolded. Students must be able to consult and follow the scaffold device as they carry out the skill. Devices or techniques scaffold thinking only if they structure it and are used by students while thinking.
>
> There are at least three teaching techniques or devices that provide the kind of specific, explicit, formative structural scaffolding appropriate for supporting student efforts to apply cognitive operations in the early stages of practice or development. These are procedural checklists, process- structured questions, and graphic organizers. Each of these techniques provides a framework of verbal and/or visual prompts that guides students through the execution of any cognitive operation. By using any of these techniques, we can scaffold initial student efforts to improve their execution of specific cognitive operations while students actually apply these operations and without our having to intervene directly in their learning. Thus, when using scaffolds, we not only provide instructive guidance to all students but we also are freed to provide personalized, individual assistance to those students who may require additional assistance. (Beyer, 1997, pp. 171–172)

The astute reader may have noticed that Thinkback is itself a form of scaffolding. The structures of thinking aloud and of working in pairs are temporary structures that are intended to be removed once the skills practiced within them become second nature. The questions asked by a good listener eventually become part of the problem solver's own way of thinking and no longer require the assistance of a listener. But Thinkback provides more than a scaffold. It also produces a *thought image* with which teachers can see inside the active minds of students and observe the details of thought in action. Teachers are able to view these *thought images*, because, as Dr. Beyer has already pointed out, "when using scaffolds, we not only provide instructive guidance to all students but we also are freed to provide personalized, individual assistance to those students who may require additional assistance." In fact, with Thinkback we are free to listen to all students: those who require additional assistance themselves and those who may provide us with the additional assistance and insight we need to grow as teachers.

WHAT IS A GRAPHIC ORGANIZER?

A graphic organizer is a tool for structuring thinking. Beyer (1997) described it as follows.

> In general, a graphic organizer is a chart or diagram that arranges the components of something in some way. It may take the form of a web, a

> pictograph, a series of boxes or columns, a matrix, or any other diagram that displays information in a visually structured manner. Students fill it in by entering the kinds of information indicated by the visual or verbal prompts embedded in the organizer. By providing a structure for the content or information it displays, such an organizer assists students in storing and then retrieving this information as well as making it meaningful and applying it. Graphic organizers are widely used in most subjects to organize information, to represent the meaning of written texts, and to describe subject-matter concepts.
>
> Graphic organizers are also extremely useful for structuring or scaffolding thinking operations. When used for this purpose, however, a graphic organizer presents a visual representation of a thinking *procedure* rather than of a product of thinking. Graphic organizers of thinking *products*, such as concept webs or hamburger paragraphs, may demand thinking to produce them but do little to help that thinking along. A graphic organizer for a thinking *procedure*, on the other hand, is one that requires and assists students to move mentally through the steps by which a particular cognitive operation can be effectively carried out. (pp. 183–186)

Beyer presented a variety of common graphic organizers; we will illustrate the use of only a few. Note that the use of these organizers is largely self-evident, thus they do not require a great deal of explanation. Students can use them "without our having to intervene directly."

A SEQUENCE FOR: ____________________

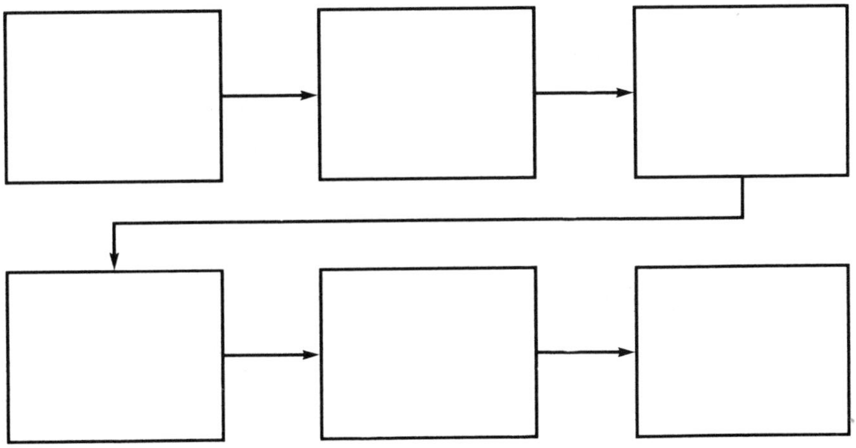

SEQUENCING

The graphic organizer for sequencing can be applied to any sequencing problem. We start with a pair of students who have been given this organizer along with a problem from *Problem Solving and Comprehension* (problem 7, p. 129). Following the problem statement there is a dialogue between a pair of students who are engaged in the roles of problem solver and listener. The dialogue provides the reader with an opportunity to experience the Thinkback process in action. To gain the most from what this book has to offer it is essential that one reads the dialog carefully, probably several times. Other parts of the book may be skimmed but the dialogues should be read in their entirety.

Problem Statement

The Great Lakes differ in both their areas (measured in square miles) and their depths. However these two dimensions do not keep step perfectly. For example, Lake Michigan is exceeded in depth only by Lake Superior, but it is exceeded in area by both Lakes Superior and Huron. Lake Superior is by far the largest and deepest of the Great Lakes, but Lake Ontario, which is the smallest in area, is deeper than both Lakes Huron and Erie. Lake Erie is larger than Lake Ontario but it is not only shallower than Huron; it is also shallower than Ontario. Show the order of the Great Lakes according to depth. (Whimbey & Lochhead, 1999, p. 131)

Problem Solution

Martha

This is very confusing. I don't know where to start.

George

Yes.

Martha

Let's see. The first sentence tells me nothing. The second only that depth and area are not perfectly related. The third says Superior is the deepest and Michigan comes next, let me write that in the boxes.

A SEQUENCE FOR: ________________

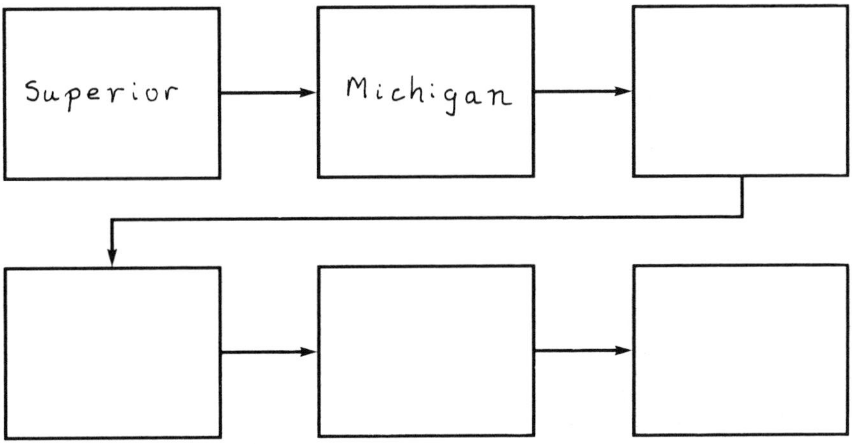

George

A good listener asks questions that will make the Problem Solver explain how graphics are being used.

Why that box?

Martha

This answer explains nothing, and George has to try another question to get Martha to talk about the graphic.

Because Superior is first it is the deepest.

George

But if it is the deepest it should have the lowest bottom—it should be lowest.

Martha has finally begun to describe how the graphic works.

Martha

Hmmmm.
No, that is not right.
The problem is with the organizer. It does not say what kind of order we are using. It just leaves that blank. I had better fill that in. So I will write in the blank "the Great Lakes from deepest to least deep."

Now, where was I?
I finished the third sentence; what does the fourth say? "... but Lake Ontario ... is deeper than both Lakes Huron and Erie." Can I use this to tell me that Ontario comes next?
How many lakes are there?

In general a Listener should not offer this kind of information. In this case it proves useful, mainly because it is wrong.

George

Six.

Martha

Six? Let me count.... Michigan, Superior, Huron, Superior, Ontario, Huron, Erie. I get seven.
No, wait ... I think I double counted.

George

What are you doing? I am getting a blurry thought image.

Martha

I am skimming the paragraph looking for names of lakes and counting each time I get a new one. Only I lost track of which were new.

Once again this is not ideal Listener behavior, but in this case it works well.

George

But you can see that there are six.

Martha

This is a reference to problem 5 on p. 131 of Problem Solving and Comprehension

See? Where?
Oh, the graphic! But the graphic doesn't know what problem we are solving. It can't know that there are six Great Lakes. We might have been working with any kind of objects say for example which movie monster is most horrible, like Dracula, Wolfman, and Mummy.

No, the graphic may have more or fewer boxes than we need. I have to count the lakes listed in the problem. I had better make a list.
Michigan, Superior, Huron, Sup ... (no cross that out), Ontario, Erie.

Michigan
Superior
Huron
Ontario
Erie

Let me check my list by reading all the names in the order they appear: Michigan, Superior, Superior, Huron, Superior, Ontario, Huron, Erie, Erie, Ontario, Huron, Ontario. There that is all of them.There are five.

George

Not six.

A SEQUENCE FOR: Great Lakes from deepest to Least deep.

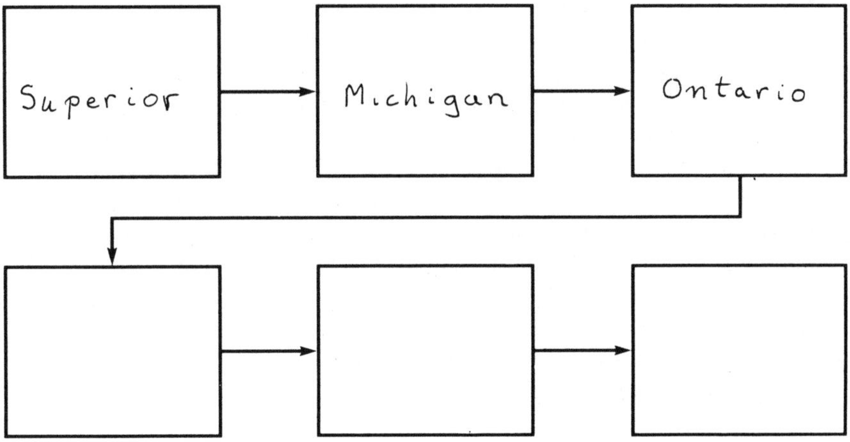

Martha

Where was I?
There are five Great Lakes and I have written in two. So if Ontario is deeper than the last two it must come next. I can write it in.

Now what comes next?"Lake Erie is larger ... but shallower than Huron." OK, so Huron comes next and then Erie.

A SEQUENCE FOR: Great Lakes from deepest to least deep.

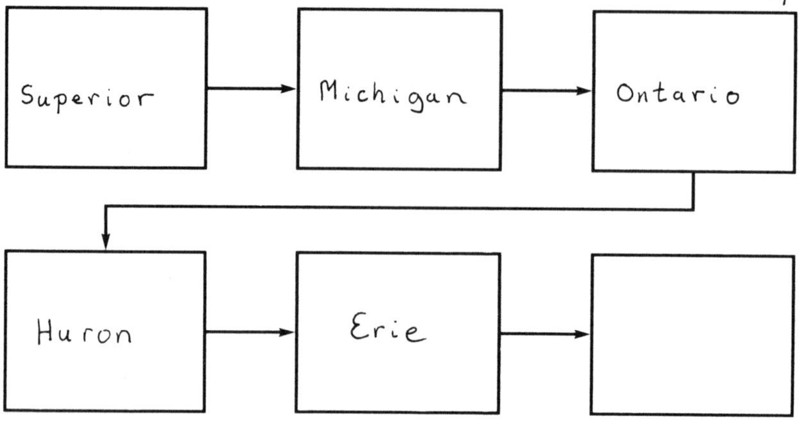

SORTING OUT THE LESSON

There are many ways to combine graphic organizers and the Thinkback strategy. In this particular case, students were given a specific organizer and a specific problem. They were not asked, as they might have been, to make or find the graphic organizer that would best serve their needs. For some reason, either poor planning or devilish cleverness, the organizer the students were given does not precisely match the situation in the problem. Under a more traditional instructional situation this mismatch might lead to confusion and frustration. In the context of Thinkback, it leads to confusion and insight. Through the dynamic of the Thinkback dialog, the students are able to move past an initial confusion caused by inconsistencies to attain a deeper understanding of the relationship between a graphic organizer and the act of organizing. To design these inconsistencies artfully, teachers must have a thorough understanding of both the students they are teaching and the material under study.

Note also that George forgets his role when he claims that there are six Great Lakes. He is intruding into the problem solver's territory. In most situations, this kind of listener behavior will disrupt the process. Fortunately, in this particular case, the listener's inappropriate contribution to the problem solver's job actually serves to advance the dialogue. One reason for the advance is that the listener's contribution is factually incorrect. This forces the problem solver to describe in detail why the listener's idea is wrong.

A MATH PROBLEM

Sequencing problems appear in many contexts. Here, we consider one from mathematics. In the dialogue that follows, we observe how two students solve the problems using the same simple graphic organizer employed in the last problem.

Problem Statement

Order the following numbers from smallest to largest.

$$5^{1/2}$$
$$357 \times 10^{-5}$$
$$0.05$$
$$1/5$$
$$0.10005$$

Problem Solution

Alpha

357×10^{-5} looks biggest to me. 357 is certainly bigger than 5.

Beta

Beta may be giving Alpha a hint here but has succesfully managed to disguise it so that it seems like a question.

What does the $\times 10^{-5}$ mean? My thought image does not show me how you are thinking about that.

Alpha

Yuk, do I need to think about that?
It means you multiply 357 by 10^{-5}.
But what does 10^{-5} mean?
I am not too sure but I remember something about moving the decimal point. I think it must be to the left because of the minus sign. And five places because of the 5. So in 357 the decimal is just to the right of the seven. I move three places and I am to the left of the three. I need to move two more places so I get 0.00357.
Now that looks like the smallest number.
I am going to put it in the bottom right box in the graphic organizer to get it out of the way.

Beta

So you can forget it.

Alpha

Alpha may be looking only at the number of places to the right and ignoring the important leftmost digits.

... so I can forget it.
Next I am going to put in 0.1005
It has four places to the right of the decimal whereas 0.00357 has five.

A SEQUENCE FOR: ________________

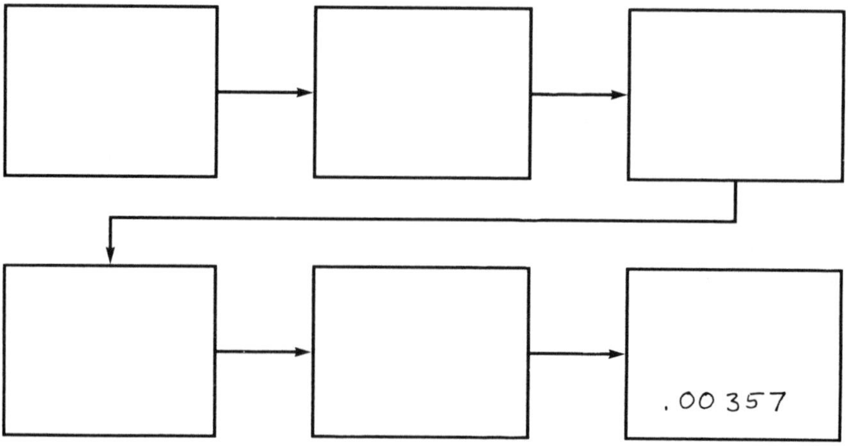

Beta

This is a very useful kind of listener response. It implies that the Problem Solver's words are understood but does not indicate whether the ideas are correct.

Ah.

Alpha

Then comes 0.05 and 1/5 and last $5^{1/2}$.

Beta

Could you explain that to me?

Alpha

I guess I should write them all the same way first so you can see it. 1/5 is the same as 2/10 which we can write as 0.2.

Beta

Yes.

Alpha

... and $5^{1/2}$ means the square root of 5. The square root of 4 is 2 so the square root of 5 is 2 and something ... like maybe 2.2.

Beta

The Listener should stop the Problem Solver whenever there is a need to check the accuracy of a step.

Wait, let me try that on my calculator. 2.2 times 2.2 is 4.84. Yes that is close to 5.

A SEQUENCE FOR: ________________

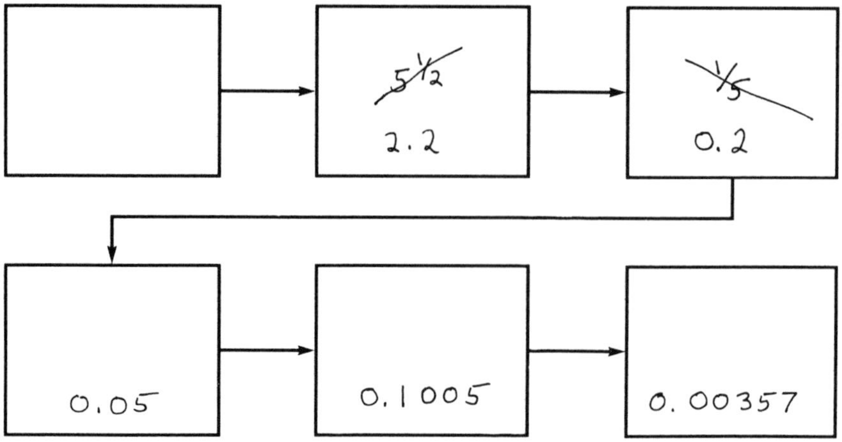

Alpha

Really? I was just guessing—that is amazing.
So now I have 2.2, 0.2, and 0.05.
The last is the smallest because it has two places to the right of the decimal. Next comes 0.2 and then 2.2.

Beta

But 2.2 has the same number of places to the right of the decimal as does 0.2 Why do you say it is bigger?

Now Beta seems to be checking out the earlier hypothesis that Alpha is only counting the number of places to the right of the decimal and ignoring the left most digits.

Alpha

Because of the 2.

Beta

Two? Which 2?

Alpha

The 2 that is a 2, the other 2 twos are really two tenths.

Beta

You have lost me.

Beta may or may not be lost. In either case this is a good way to get Alpha to explain things more carefully.

Alpha

2.2 is really 2 plus 0.2 while 0.2 is just zero plus 2/10.
So 2 plus something has to be bigger than that something alone.

Beta

... and 0.05 is smaller than 0.2 because ...

Alpha

... because it is more to the right.

Beta

Could you explain that a different way? I am not sure I get it.

Alpha

Well 0.05 is really 5/100 while 0.2 is 2/10 or 20/100.
So 5 is smaller than 20.

Beta

OK, and what is next?

Alpha

Next is 0.1005.
0.005 is smaller than 0.05.

Beta

What happened to the 0.1?

Alpha

The what?
Oh! Yes there is a problem.
0.1005 is 0.1 plus 0.0005 and 0.1 is bigger than 0.05!
Wow, this is a mess.
I need to put 0.1005 above 0.05.
I will move 2.2 and the 0.2 left one space each so there is room to write 0.1005 where the 0.2 was.
Now that leaves 0.00357 as smaller than 0.05. and it still is.

A SEQUENCE FOR: ____________

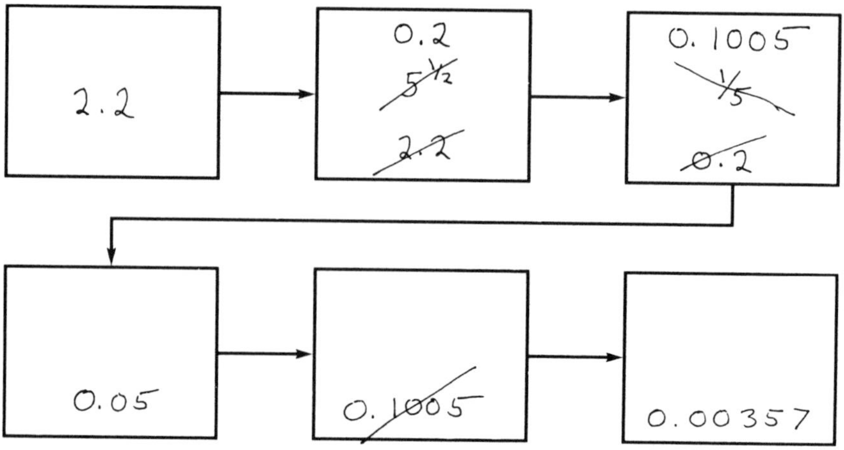

Beta

So you believe you have it?

Alpha

So I *believe* I have it, … but then I once thought 357×10^{-5} was the biggest.

COMPARING

Our students have been given the task of comparing apples and oranges using the standard Venn diagram graphic.

Linda

I was always told you can't compare apples and oranges.

COMPARING

______________ AND ______________

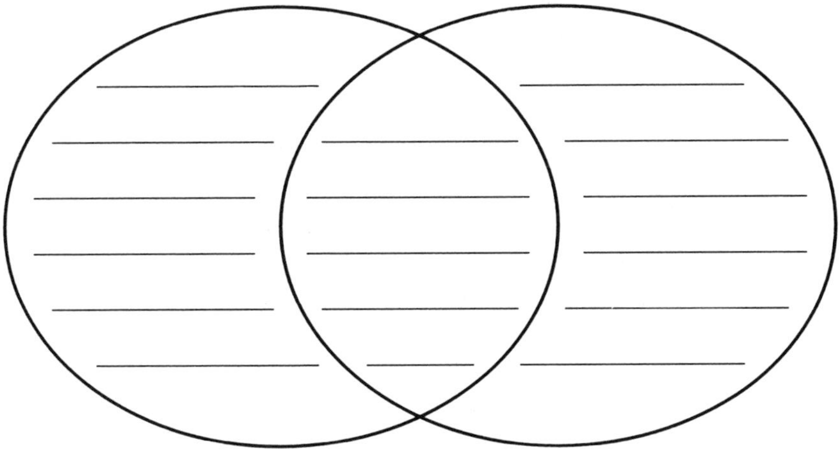

Ken

So when has "can't" stopped you.

Linda

Well they are both fruit. I will put "fruit" in the middle, since that is where you put things that are true for both.
... and they are both "good to eat." I will put that in the middle too.

But oranges are orange and apples are red. I will put "red" on the left and "orange" on the right. Oh, and I had better fill in the top blanks. We are comparing "apples" and "oranges."

COMPARING

apples AND oranges

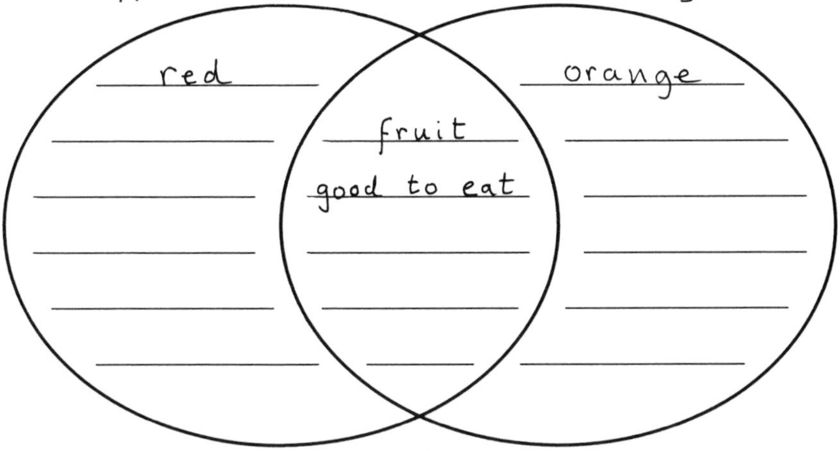

Ken

Are apples always red?

Linda

No, some are green and some are yellow. Actually they are all green to begin with ... as are oranges.
So I will put "sometimes green" in the middle.
I have been filling in all the similarities and not the differences.
So oranges have a "thick skin" and apples have a "thin skin."
Peeled apples "turn brown" and oranges "keep color."
Apples "grow where it is cold," oranges "grow where it is warm."

Ken

Is that all?

Linda

No, I could go on all day.
There is no end to this. There are seeds, juice, bugs, and pie.

Ken

Pie?

Linda

There is apple pie but no such thing as orange pie.

Ken

Not yet.

COMPARING

apples AND oranges

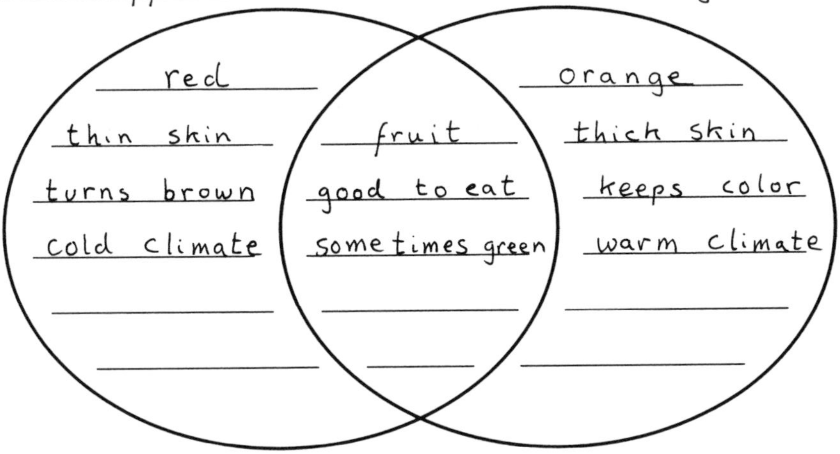

SUMMARY

This chapter has given a brief introduction to some of the ways in which the Thinkback strategy can be used in conjunction with graphic organizers. It is not intended to be a complete introduction to the use of graphic organizers; readers interested in such an introduction may find it in Beyer's book or in any of the many sources he mentions. Rather, this chapter demonstrates how Thinkback can be a useful tool for exploring new material that has not been fully defined. By not including detailed information on graphic organizers, the chapter illustrates how students can learn to use new tools and in the process construct their own instruction(s). Thinkback is not essential to this process but it is helpful in pursuing the goal of making the student generated instructions explicit and specific.

CHAPTER FOUR

For Writing Aloud

THE WHIMBEY WRITING PROGRAM

Skilled writing is mostly rewriting. A serious writer spends relatively little time creating new sentences or setting down original ideas. Instead, he or she spends most of his or her time and effort rearranging and refashioning the words and thoughts already on paper. The Whimbey Writing Program (Whimbey & Blanton, 1997) assembles a powerful collection of reformulation techniques and elaborates each with suitable skill-building exercises. In this chapter, we show how Thinkback can be applied to some of these exercises, specifically to *sentence combining* and *text reconstruction*.

We begin with exercises from *Analyze Organize Write* (Whimbey & Jenkins, 1987). This book has been largely superseded by *How to Analyze, Organize and Write Effectively* (Whimbey & Blanton, 1995). We start with the earlier work, however, because it contains some valuable *sentence combining* exercises not presented in the newer version.

SENTENCE COMBINING

Unpolished writing often contains short, choppy sentences. Sentence combining develops the skill of transforming this kind of immature writing into well-coordinated, complex sentences that are both clear and concise. Consider the following example of choppy prose: "A cat chased a lizard. The cat was big. The cat was fat.

His fur was thick." After combining these sentences we might have: "A big, fat, furry cat chased a lizard."

In order to help students move from writing choppy sentences to composing fluid prose, Dr. Whimbey uses the shaping paradigm, starting where the students are and gradually encouraging transitions to better performance. Here are two examples of *sentence combining* exercises taken from Whimbey and Jenkins (1987, p. 4). Following each problem, a Problem Solver–Listener dialogue is given, illustrating how the Thinkback strategy can be applied to exercises of this kind. Try the exercise first yourself, then read the sample dialogue. Remember that the dialogue is only an example of what might be done; it is *not* the best possible solution.

Problem

Combine the following three sentences:

The thief entered a house.
He entered it quietly.
The house was large and dark.

Problem Solver–Listener Dialogue

Problem Solver

"The thief entered a house. He entered it quietly. The house was large and dark."
The thief is going to be the subject of my sentence, he is the actor.

Listener

In order to get the Problem Solver to explain things in more detail, the Listener expresses surprise at the choice the Problem Solver has made.

Why do you say that? In the last sentence the house is the subject.

Problem Solver

The Problem Solver has not really answered the Listener's question, but is starting to talk in slightly more detail.

Hmm. I could say the house was robbed ... but that sounds awkward and is passive. I will stick with the thief.

So ...

The thief entered the house ... what kind of house?
The thief entered the large, dark house ... I am missing the second sentence.
The thief quietly entered the large, dark house.... Do I have everything?

The Problem Solver is beginning to monitor his own thinking.

From the first sentence I have: thief, entered and house
From the second sentence I have: entered and quietly
From the third sentence I have: house, large, and dark. It fits.
My answer is: The thief entered the large, dark house.

Listener

The Listener is grasping to find some question to ask. The result is a consideration of some fine points that goes well beyond the original intention of the problem.

But in the first sentence you changed *a* to *the.*

Problem Solver

You would prefer, "The thief entered a large, dark house?" That might be better; without more context I can't tell. It seems to depend on whether we are supposed to know which house or just that it is large and dark.

Listener

The second version feels a bit more mysterious to me, slightly creepy.

Problem Solver

I agree, but without knowing the full story in which this sentence fits. I still can't tell which is the better version.

SUMMARY

Notice how the dynamic of the Pair Problem Solving dialogue stimulates the PS to articulate thoughts in greater detail than would occur if the exercise had been solved by one PS working alone. Furthermore, the listener's need to find something to ask about drives the conversation to important, although subtle, areas that may well go beyond the original expectations of the exercise.

In the next example, we see how Thinkback can also assist novice writers who are in much greater need of assistance.

Problem

Combine the following four sentences:

The horse jumped over the fence.
The horse was grey.
The jump was done gracefully.
The fence was low and made of brick.

Problem Solver–Listener Dialogue

Problem Solver

"The horse jumped over the fence.
The horse was grey.
The jump was done gracefully.
The fence was low and made of brick."
The horse jumped over the fence; it was grey and graceful....

Listener

Isn't the bit after "it" like a new sentence?

Problem Solver

Hmm. Ya, I guess so.
The horse was grey and jumped over the fence which was done gracefully ... and oh yes the fence was low and made of brick.
Let me try again.
The horse was grey and jumped over the fence that was low and made of brick and was done gracefully.

Listener

The fence was graceful?

Problem Solver

No, the horse!

Listener

An excellent listener strategy is to reflect back exactly what the Problem Solver says.

The horse was graceful and grey....

Problem Solver

No, actually it was the jump that was graceful.
The horse was grey and jumped gracefully over the fence that was low and made of brick.

Listener

Do you have to start with "the horse was grey"?

Problem Solver

Why not, it was, wasn't it?

Listener

Well it is a bit confusing—it is like you have the horse doing two things ... being grey and jumping. Isn't the jumping what is important?

Problem Solver

That might be a horse of a different color.

Listener

Hiss.

Problem Solver

Hmmm. The grey horse jumped....
The grey horse jumped gracefully....
The grey horse jumped gracefully over the fence that was low and made of brick.

Listener

Good.
Can you make it any shorter?

Problem Solver

Shorter?
How about—
The grey horse jumped gracefully over the low, brick fence.

Listener

Does that have everything in it?

Problem Solver

Let me check.
It has "The horse jumped over the fence." (Points to words)
It says "the horse was grey."
It says the jump was "graceful" ... and implies it was "done."
It says the fence was low and brick.

Listener

Yes, but it does not say the fence was made of brick.

Problem Solver

Well it is implied in "low, brick fence."

Thinkback often stimulates a modest amount of competition and mutual needling. This is beneficial provided it stays friendly.

Listener

So was it made of low too?

Problem Solver

NO!
It was made low, like I am about to make you.

CREATING WORD PICTURES

Often a writer needs to help the reader imagine a scene. Extra details can make the difference between a lifeless image and one that creates a vivid image for the reader. The more vivid the image the more likely the reader will remember it.

When giving instructions, one could say, "Take your first left, go two blocks, turn right...." These instructions may be accurate, but they don't paint a picture. "Left at the Exxon station and right immediately after St. James Church" conveys the same information but creates an easy-to-remember picture.

The following exercise (from Whimbey & Blanton, 1995, pp. 2–5.) illustrates how to work with this kind of visual information.

Writing Directions for a Driver

Exercises

Instructions. If friends are coming to a party at your home or are meeting you downtown to see a movie, you might have to write driving directions. This is one of the simplest forms of description, but your directions must be clear so the drivers won't get lost.

Exercise 1 (approximately 5 minutes). The sentences on page 3 refer to the map. Number the sentences so they are arranged into directions for getting from the corner of Adams and Oak to the movie theater on Central.

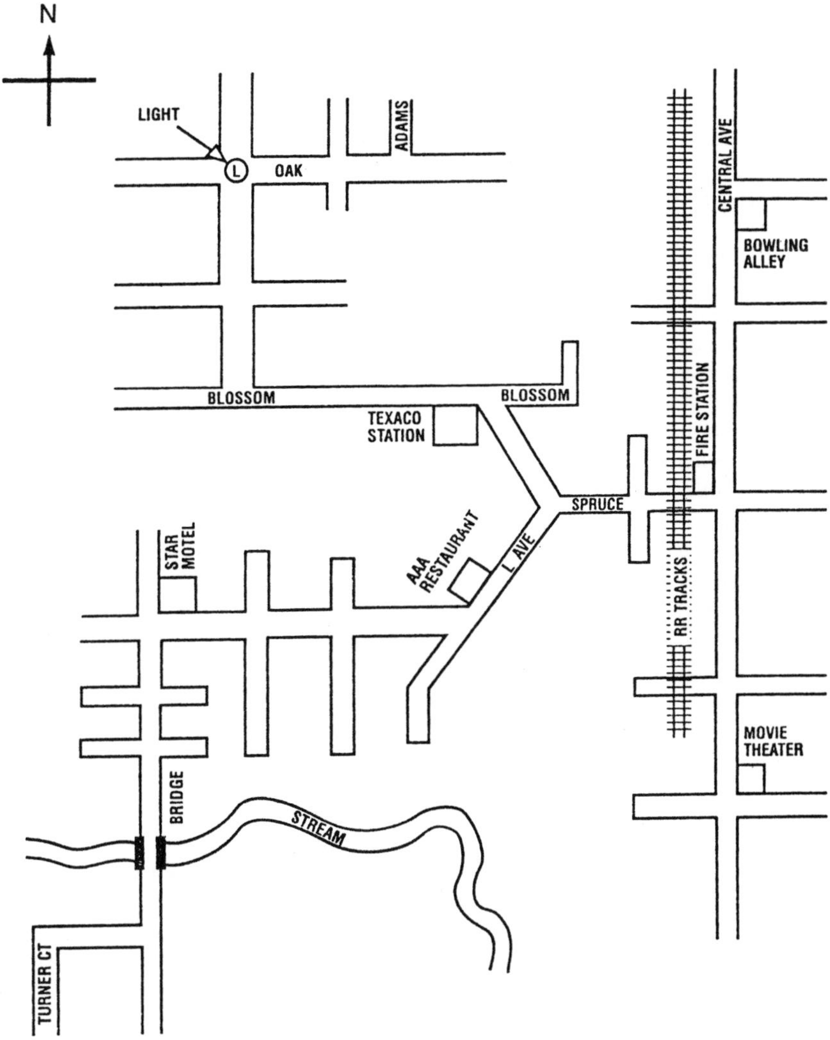

____ Go two blocks, which will bring you to the end of the road, and make a left onto Blossom.

____ You will come to a fork in the road, where you should take the left branch, putting you on Spruce.

____ When you get to the Texaco station, bear right onto L Avenue.

____ Drive for two blocks and you will see the movie theater.

____ Drive west along Oak Street to the first light and then make a left.

____ Go straight until you pass over the railroad tracks, and then make a right at the next corner.

Problem Solver–Listener Dialogue

In this problem the Problem Solver has to look both at the sentences and at the map. This changing focus of attention makes the logic of the dialog more complex and difficult to follow. Readers of this dialog must remain active and alert if they are to follow the logic.

Problem Solver

So we need to go from Adams and Oak to the movie theater. Let me see, where are these places on the map?

Listener

What are you looking at?

The Problem Solver is looking at the map and tracing out possible paths

Problem Solver

I am trying to find Adams or Oak.
There is Oak (points) at the top of the page, and Adams comes right down into it. Now I need to find the movie theater.
I see Blossom, Texaco, AAA, Star, bridge, wrong way, nothing here. Back up to Spruce, Fire Station, Bowling ... no, go down. Ah! Movie Theater, I found it!

Listener

Yes.

Now the Problem Solver has shifted attention to the sentences

Problem Solver

Ok, now I go back to Oak and Adams. I need to find a sentence which gives me instructions starting from here. "Go two blocks." It doesn't say in which direction. I need a sentence to get oriented.

Listener

What do you mean oriented?

Problem Solver

The Problem Solver now skims sentences looking for one with orientation instructions.

I need a sentence that tells me how to start moving from the corner of Oak and Adams. If I go straight up I will fall off the map.

The Problem Solver is now looking at the map.

"You will come to a fork" ... no.
"When you get" ... no.
"Drive for two blocks" ... no.
"Drive west" ... maybe, looks good but let me check the last one.
"Go straight," no.
So let me read this sentence fully.
"Drive west along Oak (good I am on Oak!) to the first light and then make a left."
Where is the first light?
There it is! Is it west of Oak and Adams?

Listener

Wait my thought image is blurry. How would you know that?

Problem Solver

North is usually up but, ah over on the upper left corner there is an arrow pointing to N. I think that is a compass-like thing. Now, where is West? When I look at a map of the U.S., Canada is on top (that is north). And the West Coast is to the left and the East coast is to the right. So left is west.
And, yes, going left along Oak is going west.

Listener

What if you didn't have a compass?

Problem Solver

The Problem Solver has responded to the question as though the task were to give instructions rather than simply to put the sentences in their correct order.

Well, I would tell him to look up and down the street and go towards the light, but that is not our task here. I am only supposed to order the sentences as given, not improve them.

The Problem Solver starts to number the sentences.

So what comes next? Wait. First I put a "1" next to "Drive west." Let me look at the map. I want to go down two blocks to Blossom; that is South.

The Problem Solver is careful to double check the choice for the second sentence.

"Go two blocks ... " (looks good) "which will bring you to the end of the road, and take a left onto Blossom." Great!
But wait, I forgot. Did the first sentence point us south at the light?"

I had better check.
It says "make a left."
Yes, that is south.

Listener

Wait a minute! I have a blurry image.
You just said left was West. Now you say it is South?

Problem Solver

Yup.
The left side of the map is West, when North is at the top.
But if you are traveling West and turn left (by 90 degrees), you will be facing South.

Listener

OK.

Problem Solver

So I can put a "2" next to the sentence "Go two blocks.... "Where is the next sentence?
Looking at the map....
I need to be going east on Blossom, and the last turn headed me that way so I just keep going until the Texaco. OK, which sentence has Texaco?
Here it is!
"When you get to the Texaco station, bear right onto L Avenue."
L Avenue! I don't see any L Avenue!
Oh? There it is, down below. Some L, looks more like a hockey stick.
So I put a "3" at "When you get...."

Listener

So where are you?

Problem Solver

I am here (points).
Just past the Texaco. I will need to turn onto Spruce and cross the railway.
Do any of the sentences mention those?"
You will come to a fork ... on Spruce" This is it.
"You will come to a fork in the road, where you should take the left branch, putting you on Spruce." Yes, that is correct. I put a "4" before "You will...."

Listener

How do you know that is correct? You haven't looked at any of the other sentences. Perhaps one of them is better.

Problem Solver

How could that be?
This sentence takes me from where I am to where I want to be. Any other sentence would have to take me nowhere or it would take me to the wrong place.

Listener

There might be a sentence warning you to lock your doors because Godzilla hangs out near Spruce.

Problem Solver

Well, there isn't, and if there were I could deal with it at the end. ... only it would be a pain to renumber, but I am pretty sure there isn't any such sentence.
So, I am on L. No, I am on Spruce!
Looking at the map ...
I need to cross the tracks, pass the fire station, and turn right.
"Drive two blocks ..." no.
"Go straight until you pass over the railroad tracks, (Yes!) and then make a right at the next corner." Got it!
I put a "5" next to
"Go Straight ... "
And now there is only one left, it must be "6."

Listener

Are you certain?

Problem Solver

I am certain. But I will read it just to be sure there is no Godzilla. "Drive for two blocks and you will see the movie theater."

Hmm.
If I really drive two blocks, the movie theater will be in my rear view mirror. Not very good instructions.

Listener

Perhaps there is a Godzilla?

SUMMARY

Notice that the previous dialogue has made the problem much longer and more complicated than it might otherwise have been. Because Thinkback is designed to improve thinking skills, it often converts simple problems into quite complex problems. Students learn a great deal more from such problems than they otherwise might, but they often take much longer to complete the exercises. In our view, this extra time is a wise investment.

Spending the extra time can be either an unaffordable luxury or an absolute necessity. The choice depends on whether you are preparing students for a world with surprises and unanticipated turns or a straightforward world with no Godzillas.

Reordering jumbled sentences, as in the previous example, is one instance of text reconstruction, a technique which many great writers have used to hone their own craft.

TEXT RECONSTRUCTION

Text reconstruction is a technique based on strategies writers such as Benjamin Franklin and Jack London used to develop their writing skills (for more details see Linden & Whimbey, 1990a, p. 39). Text reconstruction involves taking jumbled sentences and putting them in their most meaningful order. The exercise allows one to focus on how the sequence and logic of a presentation are composed without having to be distracted by the necessity of paying attention to grammar and other similar details.

In the section on Creating Word Pictures, we encountered Text Reconstruction in a specific case where the logic of the paragraph is dictated by a map. This situation has the advantage of having pictorial representation (a graphic organizer) to help guide the logic that describes the order of the sentences within the paragraph.

In the purer forms of Text Reconstruction, there is no visual guide to the logic. The order of the sentences is determined by the rhetoric of the paragraph. This includes the logic of the argument being made in the paragraph and the grammatical structure of the sentences employed. For example, a sentence beginning with the word "thus" can only follow one or more sentences in which an argument has been made. It can never be the opening sentence of a new topic.

Here is an example from *The Whimbey Writing Program* (p. 41):

___ Finally, because of increased real estate and heating costs, houses and apartments have become smaller.
___ First, the majority of working-age American adults hold jobs, so they don't have time to care for an aged parent.
___ In earlier times, and still in places such as China, the elderly were cared for in the families of their grown children.
___ There is no longer an extra room for Grandma.
___ But this is no longer the case in America for several reasons.
___ Second, American families are highly mobile, moving frequently to obtain better jobs or other benefits.
(*Vocabulary Tip: mobile—moving often, able to move.*)
___ This divides families by hundreds or even thousands of miles, rather tha leaving adult children near their elderly parents.

Exercise 2 (approximately 5 minutes). Write the sentences in the order you numbered them to form a paragraph stating a problem and three causes.

____

____

____

____

____

____

____

____

____

____

Problem Solver–Listener Dialogue

Problem Solver

I need to find the first sentence.
It will not be the one starting with "Finally."
Nor do I think it will be the one starting with "First"; that would be an awkward way to start a paragraph.
"In earlier times," is a good opening. I will look at the rest to see if there is another option.
"There is no longer room for Grandma." That would be an interesting opening, but a bit abrupt.
"But ... " is no way to start a paragraph.

Listener

The Problem Solver has been rejecting sentences without giving any reasons. The Listener uses this question to ask for more detail.

Wait, I am getting a blurry image. Why do you say "but" is no good?

Problem Solver

Because it has to contradict something that was said before. And there is nothing that comes before the first sentence.
"Second," is not an opening, it needs to come after "first." "This divides...."
This needs to refer to something earlier.
So I think I will start by placing a "1" next to "In earlier times, and still in places such as China, the elderly were cared for in the families of their grown children." That is a good opening sentence.

Listener

The Listener is reflecting back the uncertainty the Problem Solver expressed earlier.

Why is it better than "There is no longer room for Grandma?"

Problem Solver

I am not absolutely sure that it is better. But I am going to start with it and see what happens.
Now, I remember there was a "First...."
"First the majority of working-age American adults hold jobs.... "
This is explaining something but there is nothing yet that needs to be explained. Let me see if there is a second sentence that asks to be explained.
How about "But this is no longer the case in America for several reasons."
This sentence can follow the first sentence and it asks for a laying out of reasons ... first, second, third. I will put a "2" next to "But this is...."

Listener

The Listener may understand what the Problem Solver is doing but nevertheless find it helpful to claim confusion as a means of getting the Problem Solver to talk more explicitly.

The image is blurry again. Why does it follow the first?

Problem Solver

The first sentence says that in earlier times kids took care of their parents. The second sentence says this is no longer the case in America. The two go together.

Listener

Here the Listener moves beyond the traditional role and comes close to directing what the Problem Solver should do.

Which is the key idea for the paragraph? Isn't that supposed to be the topic sentence and the first sentence in the paragraph?

Problem Solver

Let's see.
"In earlier times ..." seems to set the stage. The key idea is that we no longer do this in America. So in this case the topic sentence comes second. You can't put them the other way around; it doesn't work. You can't start a paragraph with "But."

Listener

The Listener wisely decides to drop the diversion.

Hmmm.

Problem Solver

Pay attention! The text here is difficult to follow because the sentence starting with the word "second" is not the second sentence but rather the fourth.

So now I need to find the third sentence, but I already argued that would be "First, the majority of working-age American adults hold jobs, so they don't have time to care for an aged parent." I will put a "3" next to "First, ..." and perhaps second goes next. "Second, American families are highly mobile, moving frequently to obtain better jobs or other benefits."

Listener

Are you sure this is next?

Problem Solver

No, not really.
I had better check that nothing fits in between.
It is not "Finally because of increased real estate...."

Nor is it "There is no longer an extra room for Grandma."
"This divides families by hundreds or even thousands of miles, rather than leaving adult children near their elderly parents."
That does not fit either, but it does fit right after number "4."
First, I had better put a "4" next to "Second ... " and then a "5" next to "This divides."
What is next?
I do not remember any "Third."

Oh, here is "Finally...." Let us try that.
"Finally, because of increased real estate and heating costs, houses and apartments have become smaller."
That fits. I will put a "6" next to "Finally...."

Listener

But what about Grandma?

Problem Solver

Yes, we have left her out in the cold.
Does she fit at the end?
"There is no longer an extra room for Grandma." Yes, that does work. It is not what I expected, but it works. Grandma is number "7."

SUMMARY

In this chapter, we have glanced at three kinds of reformulation exercises: sentence combining, reorganizing instructions to fit a map and text reconstruction—the reordering of sentences to make a coherent paragraph. Additional information on these reformulation techniques can be found at www.tracinstitute.com. Many more such exercises are found in Whimbey's writing texts: *Analyze Organize, Write*; *How to Analyze, Organize, and Write Effectively*; and *Analytical Writing and Thinking*; *Mastering Reading Through Reasoning*; *Analytical Reading and Reasoning*; and *Keys to Quick Writing Skills*. Although these books do not require the use of the Thinkback strategy, each has been written to be consistent with its application. The combination of Thinkback and these carefully constructed shaping exercises greatly enhance student learning while, at the same time, reducing many aspects of the teacher's instructional load. The self-correcting and self-focusing aspects of the Listener–Problem Solver dynamic frees teachers from having to deal with many small issues that otherwise would dominate the classroom discourse. This time can now be used to work with students who are falling behind and really need expert guidance.

CHAPTER FIVE

Kneading Knowledge As Design

THE DESIGN OF KNOWLEDGE

In *Knowledge As Design*, Dr. David Perkins (1986) pointed out that the traditional view of knowledge is static and lifeless. "Knowledge as information purveys a passive view of knowledge, one that highlights knowledge in storage rather than knowledge as an implement of action" (p. 5). To contrast this, Dr. Perkins suggested that we view knowledge as a tool designed by humans for specific purposes. "The theme of knowledge as design can break the familiar frame of reference, opening up neglected opportunities for understanding and critical and creative thinking" (pp. 2–3).

Dr. Perkins proposed a simple four step process for implementing this new perspective. It involves asking four simple questions about the object or concept we wish to understand:

1. What is its purpose (or purposes)?
2. What is its structure?
3. What are model cases of it?
4. What are arguments that explain and evaluate it? (Perkins, 1986, p. 5)

Most of *Knowledge As Design* provides examples in a wide variety of different contexts of how these four questions can be posed and answered. Here, we illustrate what might happen if two students were asked to apply the principles of Thinkback to the task of answering these questions.

Several topics are suggested by Dr. Perkins as suitable examples of concepts that can be illuminated by the four Knowledge as Design questions. We consider three:

1. The organization of the U. S. Senate.
2. The organization of a paragraph.
3. The rate × time = distance formula. (Perkins, 1986, p. 9)

Because of the rich and open-ended nature of these questions the dialogues they generate are longer and more complex than those for traditional academic short questions. The dialogues presented in the next section are not intended to represent ideal solutions, but rather to show how students with limited experience and knowledge might use the combination of Thinkback and Knowledge As Design to further their own understanding.

THE ORGANIZATION OF THE U.S. SENATE

Alpha

In this exercise, the students have not been given detailed instructions on how to apply the Thinkback strategy. They have been left to make up their own rules.

I will go with the first design question and then you can take the second.

Beta

OK

Alpha

Knowledge as Design Question 1.

So, What are the purposes of the U.S. Senate?

To give the President a hard time.
To pass laws.
To recommend federal judges, I think?

Beta

Why do you say that?

Alpha

I seem to remember hearing on the news that some federal judge was recommended by one of our state's senators. But to be honest I am not really sure.

Beta

Is that the whole Senate or just one senator?

Alpha

One senator, I think.
... the Senate also does something with foreign treaties ... can pass or veto them.
... then there is filibustering.

Beta

Here Beta is coming close to organizing Alpha's activity. The addition of the expression "I am not getting a clear thought image." helps to turn control back to Alpha.

So where is this all going? Do you have a plan or do you see a pattern? How are you thinking about this? I am not getting a clear thought image.

Alpha

Have a plan??
No, I am just rambling. I am just trying to see if I know anything.
... But I guess the overall issue is one of helping to govern the country ... only in many cases the Senate seems to be more designed to stop things from happening than to make them happen....

Beta

Beta has probably cut off this discussion too quickly. Much more could have been said.

Maybe I should take my turn at the second question and we can come back later if needed?

Alpha

Good idea.

Beta

Knowledge as Design Question 2.

What is the structure of the Senate?

I know there are two senators per state or 100 senators all together. There is a leader of some sort.... In the house it is Speaker, what is it called in the Senate? Hmm ... I think it is Majority Leader.

Alpha

What does structure mean in this context?

Beta

Good question.
How many people, how they are organized, who is in charge? ...
The Vice President fits in here somewhere.
What rules they use. When do they meet, where do they meet, ...
Then there are the two parties. The Senate is divided into two parties that always fight with each other.

Alpha

Are the two parties part of the structure or did that just happen? Can't there be three or more parties?

Beta

Well, they are sure part of the structure now. But yes, I guess that is not written into law. I don't know how the parties are written in. They must be written in in some way or else how could you have a majority and minority leader? There is a lot here I don't understand.... Why don't you try Question 3?

Alpha

Knowledge as Design Question 3.

What are model cases of it?

There is only one U.S. Senate. Only one model case and that is hardly a model.... It is the real thing. Let me see, has any country copied it? Did we base it on some previous model ... perhaps the House of Lords in England? Why did we invent it in the first place?

Beta

Good question!

Alpha

So why did I think the House of Lords might be a similar thing? It is in England and we were an English colony, but that is not much of a reason. No, it is because the House of Lords does not represent all the people—it represents the landed gentry. The senate does not represent all the people; it represents the states. So if I am looking for other examples I should look for countries that came together like the original 13 colonies and needed to give unrepresentative power to each state. I don't know what Canada has done. Russia has lots of different pieces that argue, but I am not sure how the Russian government is organized. Then there is Bosnia, but whatever they have does not seem to be working ... not that the Senate works all that well. Well, I rambled on ... I don't think I know what are other model cases, but it would be interesting to find out.

Beta

What about instances instead of model cases?

Alpha

Instances?
You mean like particular times the Senate was in session? There is the joint session with the House of Representatives for the State of the Union message. That is rather unusual. I think in the typical session no one is there. They are all out investigating social services in St. Thomas while one or two stay behind to drone on for C-Span. But I guess the typical session the politicians want you to think about is one where there is some important debate followed by a critical vote. Then everyone has to hang around for the vote. But I wonder how often that happens. I remember when there is a committee investigating something they keep interrupting so Senators can go off and vote. So they have some system where they get warned of the votes in advance. I am not sure why anyone needs to stay to hear debates.

Beta

Knowledge as Design Question 4.

Well, shall I do the last one, What are arguments that explain and evaluate it? This is a strange sort of question.

On the theme of what you were saying a while back: the senate helps to increase state power. Vermont can cancel out the vote of New York. I guess there was a good argument for that when the country first came together—otherwise the smaller states might not have joined up. But I am not sure if there is a good argument for that system today....
An argument for the filibuster system is that it protects minority opinions from being squashed by majority opinion. But that also means majority opinion often is stifled by a small number of stubborn thugs.

Alpha

Listeners often reflect back what the problem solver says. This goes a bit beyond reflecting but it does not seriously disrupt the problem solver's thinking.

Sometimes one thug.

Beta

Usually that makes me very mad, but I remember there was some issue recently when I was rather happy.
So one argument that evaluates the senate negatively is that it slows down progress. I suppose the other side of that is that it adds stability.

Alpha

Here Alpha has clearly gone beyond the listener role.

Maybe that is why the senators have longer terms; we forgot to mention that when we discussed structure. Are there arguments that help explain how the Senate works or why we have it?

Beta

Maybe a purpose of the senate is to add stability.... To slow down change.
We are getting off the question and moving back to earlier questions....
Or are we? This "arguments to explain" bit is so much like the first question about purpose.
What other arguments can I think of??? There must be lots.
The Senate allows the House pass all sorts of stupid laws because they know those laws will be changed in conference committee. Is this a good thing or not?

Alpha

This statement is in part reflecting back the spirit of Beta's comment. It also adds content to the discussion but does so in such a provocative manner that it leaves Beta in control of the problem.

Maybe it is for people who want to see stupid laws passed?

Beta

You mean like lobbyists?
I wonder who else benefits.... Sometimes a representative needs to vote for something stupid to get votes back home but does not really want to see the bill pass. I guess the senate can help then.

Alpha

Here Alpha has clearly dropped out of the listener role. From here on the two students are engaged in

So why then do we have two bodies, the House and the Senate? What arguments explain that?
It can't be that the purpose was to support lobbyists. Nor was it so the two bodies could cancel each other out.

discussion that no longer follows the rules of Thinkback.

Beta

Or one group be in St. Thomas while the other worked?

Alpha

Maybe, I expect most of the framers figured they themselves would be in the Senate. But we didn't have St. Thomas then, did we?
So why two? Well, the House represents the people while the Senate represents the States. The original colonies were rather worried about getting together, and the small states did not want to be overpowered by the big ones. The Senate helps to protect the smaller states.

Beta

So why not three?

Alpha

Three? Three what? Three legislative bodies, the House, the Senate and the Whajumacallit?
Good question? Who else needs to be represented? There is the people, the states and....

Beta

The animals, the lakes and rivers ... the Indians.

Alpha

The Indians ... the African slaves. I guess in the minds of the framers those people did not count.
Nor did women, they couldn't vote. The framers could have designed a special body for any of these groups. So the existence of only one Senate shows who had power and who did not.
You know this is getting very complicated and confusing. There is a lot we don't know or understand. Perhaps we should design some questions to research before we try to do any more with this.

Alpha

The students are clearly familiar with a tactic used in Problem-Based Learning of framing question in class that can be researched during home work.

Study questions?

Beta

Yes.
Like: How are the parties regulated in the Senate?
What would happen if every senator was his or her own party?

Alpha

Are there any other bodies like the Senate?
What countries have copied the U.S. Senate? Why did they? Does it work?

Beta

What does the Vice President do?
Did the founding fathers really plan to have the Senate slow things down?
Did they think about the Native Americans or the African slaves?

Alpha

Perhaps we have done enough....

Beta

... for one night.

REVIEW OF DIALOGUE

Notice how the four questions complement each other. Issues raised by one question help fill out the answers to other questions. Describing the structure of the Senate as having two senators from each state suggests that part of the purpose of the Senate is to represent the states. Notice, too, how the structure of

Thinkback encourages the two students to expand and elaborate their limited knowledge into a deeper understanding. By asking for clarification or by providing encouragement for a line of thought, the listener helps the problem solver expand ideas. The students began with answers that were shallow and in which they had little confidence. By the end of the session, they have posed some deep questions for further investigation, and they appear to have developed a real interest in the topic. All this has happened without any input from a teacher. Although at the beginning of the dialogue the students were not prepared to benefit much from a teacher's knowledge, by the end of the session they are primed and ready to learn from either a teacher or a textbook.

The relaxed structure employed by the students in this example eventually blurs the distinction between problem solver and listener. At one point, the students reverse roles in midproblem. In another, they act as dual problem solvers. This example shows how experienced students can beneficially move in and out of the Thinkback strategy. For novice students, however, it is important to insist on a strict adherence to proper role behavior, at least until such time as both roles have been thoroughly mastered.

THE ORGANIZATION OF A PARAGRAPH

Alpha

What is the purpose of a paragraph?

Beta

To confuse students.

Alpha

You may be right. I am sure some paragraphs are written with that purpose in mind. But I hope not all. A paragraph is supposed to make a single main point. It has a topic sentence....

Beta

That is structure not purpose.

Alpha

... and you are not acting like a listener.

Beta

Oops.

Alpha

The purpose of a paragraph should be to help the reader understand what is being said ... or perhaps to help the writer help the reader to understand. A subpurpose is to help make things clearer by breaking things into smaller parts. Perhaps it also helps the writer avoid rambling all over the place by trying to make everything in a single paragraph consistent with the main idea.

Beta

Here Beta uses the concept of the thought image to reformulate what would otherwise have been seen as a hint.

So my thought image says that you are thinking: "if being organized on a big scale is too hard—at least you can be organized on a small scale."

Alpha

Yes, and its not just organization. If you have to write a paragraph about one idea it makes you say more about that idea and not just run on to the next thing without explaining what you mean ... and now I think it is your turn to try structure.

Beta

What is the structure of a paragraph?
A paragraph has a beginning, middle, and end. The first sentence should tell you what the paragraph is about. The other sentences should elaborate and the last sentence summarize.

Alpha

Is that always true?

Beta

No, but it is the sort of thing they tell you in school.
What do I really know?
A paragraph is visually set off with blank space before and after and perhaps an indent for the first sentence. Some paragraphs tell you right away what they are about but others do not. I need to have some examples.... But I think that is your job.

Alpha

Cle - ver!
What are model cases of paragraphs?
I don't know many paragraphs I can recite from memory. I think I need to look for examples in a book. Perhaps we can use this book? Here is one:

> In Knowledge As Design David Perkins points out that the traditional view of knowledge is static and lifeless. "Knowledge as Information purveys a passive view of knowledge, one that highlights knowledge in storage rather than knowledge as an implement of action." To contrast this Perkins suggests that we view knowledge as a tool designed by humans for specific purposes. "The theme of knowledge as design can break the familiar frame of reference, opening up neglected opportunities for understanding and critical and creative thinking." (this volume, p. 66)

Beta

Here Beta deliberately shifts from listener to problem solver by moving the discussion back to the previous question.

So going back one question—the first sentence makes the main point. The second sentence illustrates it by quoting from the source. The third sentence extends the idea of the first sentence and the last sentence illustrates some of the third sentence.

Alpha

Yes, but couldn't you say the third sentence is the main idea and the first sentence sets the stage for it.

Beta

I guess so ... nothing is very straightforward. But maybe you picked a bad example. It had two quotations and only two author written sentences.

Alpha

Alpha returns to the problem solver role.

So, it is back to model cases?

Let's try a paragraph from this beat-up old book:

> The ability to analyze complex material and solve problems is a skill—just like any other skill such as the ability to play golf or the ability to drive an automobile. However, there is a peculiar difficulty involved in teaching analytical skill. Generally there are two phases to teaching a skill. First the skill is demonstrated to the student. Then the student is guided and corrected while practicing. For example, golf is taught by showing the beginner how to grasp the club, how to place his feet, how to move his arms and his body as he swings. The beginner can watch a golf pro—he can even watch a slow motion film of the pro in action—and in this way can learn the pro's technique. Furthermore, the pro can observe the beginner as he practices, he can point out his flaws, and he can show him how to improve. (Whimbey & Lochhead, 1999, p. 21)

Beta

So why did you pick that example? My *thought* image is blank.

Alpha

I am not sure I know. I guess because it was average size. Some paragraphs are short, even just one sentence long. Others are long, a page or more. But most are like this one, about a quarter page long.... Need any more examples?

Beta

I guess not.

Beta

So now I have to come up with arguments that explain and justify the paragraph.
Give me a break.

Alpha

Could you say more about that?

Beta

More about what?—break? ... Oh, I guess the paragraph does give you a break. For one thing it breaks up the page so it is not just all ink. If you are reading and you look up and lose your place, it is much easier to find it if you remember which paragraph you were in. But usually you don't have to remember whether it was the third or fifth paragraph. Your eyes sort of remember the shape or the size of the paragraph. If there were no paragraphs or if they were all the same length, it would be much harder.

Alpha

Alpha summarizes and reflects Beta's comments.

So paragraphs give your eyes a break.

Beta

Yes, and earlier we talked about how they help the reader and the writer from getting lost in too big an idea. Reading or writing one paragraph at a time helps keep the mind focused on one manageable thought.

Alpha

Alpha moves outside the listener role but for the purpose of getting Beta to talk in more detail.

Yes, that makes sense, but I still think there is more. If we had no sentences, or if sentences ran on for 10 pages or more, we would get hopelessly confused. But from what you have said so far I don't see paragraphs as essential; they are sort of nice but we could make do without them.

Beta

Beta does not respond to Alpha's prod.

That sounds right to me. I don't think any one but English teachers really need them.

Alpha

Alpha tries another approach to get Beta to describe thoughts in more detail.

Where did paragraphs come from?
Who invented them?
When?

Beta

This is part of arguments that explain and evaluate?
I have never thought about those questions.

Alpha

Me neither.

Beta

Well, before writing there was speech. Does speech have paragraphs? Sometimes you have to stop to catch your breath or to let your mind get caught up with what you are saying.

Alpha

Or you just get interrupted.

Beta

Alpha and Beta have discovered that to go into more detail they will need more factual information. They have framed several questions for further investigation. These could become the focus of independent study projects or of a special lecture from the teacher.

But in writing you can't get interrupted.
Perhaps paragraphs came about because the writer wanted to indicate a pause to let the reader respond.... Only there was no way for the writer to hear that response.
There are so many arguments here; we don't know enough to work with any of them. What is the history of the paragraph? Do the earliest writers use them? Are they used the same way in all languages? Has the function of the paragraph changed with time and with technology, printing, computers, and so on. If we knew a little about any of these questions we could make much better arguments about the function and value of paragraphs.

THE RATE TIMES TIME EQUALS DISTANCE FORMULA

Alpha

Knowledge as Design Question 1.

So what is the purpose of the formula distance equals rate times time? It is so you can find how far you went. That is assuming you know how fast you were going and how long you traveled.

Or you might use it to find out how long it was going to take to go to some place when you know how far away it is and how fast you can travel.

Beta

How do you know how fast you can go?

Alpha

Usually there is a speed limit or....
And you can use the formula to calculate how fast you are going if you know how far you went and how long it took.

Beta

That sounds like circular reasoning to me—I use how far I went to find how fast I went and how fast I went to calculate how far.

Alpha

Alpha's wisecrack serves to reflect back Beta's comments.

Well, if you are going in a circle it can be very confusing, because you can be going very fast and still end up exactly where you started.

Beta

Knowledge as Design Question 2.

So what do you think they mean by the structure of the formula —distance equals rate times time?

Beta refocuses the question.

In what sense does a formula have a structure?

Alpha

Alpha ponders Beta's question.

How about the equal sign?

Beta has switched to the problem solver role.

Beta

Yes, there is always an equals sign.... And usually one letter or variable to the left of it and several on the right. In this case we have distance on the left and rate times time on the right. I suppose that you could say the structure of rate times time is different from rate plus time or rate minus time. So if this is what we mean by structure I would say the structure of the formula is one of multiplication.

Alpha is acting more or less like a listener, but is also attempting to expand Beta's focus.

Alpha

You know what is weird about the structure; it is not balanced. An equal sign is supposed to mean balanced but there is all this stuff on the right side and only one thing on the left, it is not visually balanced. Why is that?

Beta

You are right. It is weird.The two sides aren't really equal. You wouldn't say 5 = x; you would say x = 5. So what is on the right side is like ... like the value of what is on the left. You can't say the value of 5 is x because we know the value of 5 is 5.

Alpha gives a friendly prod to keep Beta thinking.

Alpha

But x could be anything; including sometimes 5.

Beta

Right.
So the structure of the equation is that the right side is all the actions you have to do to calculate the value of the left side. At least that is the case here. But that is not always the case. We could divide both sides of the distance formula by rate. Then we get:

distance/rate = time.

Now the left side is the calculation and the right side is the answer.

Alpha confirms Beta's point.

Alpha

And 5 = x.

Beta

I am afraid so.
It seems mathematics isn't very consistent. At least not in structure. We had better move on to the examples before we get completely confused.

Alpha

Knowledge as Design Question 3.

There are lots of examples of rate times time formula.

For cars driving down the highway the distance they go is equal to rate times time. But it also works for getting things done. If I am writing paragraphs at a rate of two paragraphs per hour then the distance (measured in paragraphs) is rate times time. If I write for four hours I will write 2 times 4 paragraphs or 8 all together.

Beta

What ever made you think of that?

Alpha

If I am reading 45 pages per hour then the distance into the book (measured in pages) will be given by 45 times the number of hours I read.

Need any more examples? ...

Beta

Knowledge as Design Question 4.

What are arguments to explain formulas?

Most people don't like them; they seem very confusing. This one is actually rather simple and not so bad, but somehow when you write it as a formula it gives me the creeps.... I guess it is useful to know if things go together by adding or by multiplying (I am thinking back to what we said for the structure question). I suppose an argument for formulas is that they help you see which mathematical operations are involved.

Alpha

Strictly speaking, this is a leading

Can you think of other ways they help?

question and not good listener behavior. But it can also be viewed as an attempt to get Beta to talk in more detail.

Beta

... Not easily.Perhaps when you put numbers into a calculator, the formula helps tell you how to do it. And I guess there are those programmable things—you put in a formula and then it remembers and does the same calculation over and over for different numbers.

Alpha

That sounds a bit vague to me. My thought image is getting blurry.

Beta

Well, suppose I have to do lots of distance equals rate times time problems. If I put in the formula then I only have to enter the time and I get the distance right away.

Alpha

Alpha is needling Beta in order to ask for more detail.

A BIG savings! ... if the rate is always the same.

Beta

Well if it is more complicated it is a bigger savings.... And then there are those spread sheet things. I don't know much about them but I have seen someone entering formulas for the columns so you don't have to recalculate each entry. It seems to be pretty important in business.

Alpha

This confirms Beta's comment.

And just about everything else.

Beta

So that is the value of equations—makes calculations easier and faster (unless you get completely confused). But what arguments explain the intent and the logic?
I guess they save ink. If you write out all the words it takes much longer. Perhaps being shorter than lots of words makes it easier to see what the important parts are. I don't know; is

r x t

clearer than

rate times time?

I guess it may be, especially since "times time" is awfully confusing to look at. But I still think part of the argument that explains equations is that only certain people can read them. It is like a special language that math-types use to keep themselves above the rest of us.

Alpha

You mean like all other kinds of jargon: doctor talk, legalese, the new words young kids invent?

Beta

Oh! I forgot the most important reason. In movies when you have a scientist and they want to show how smart she is, they always have formulas on the blackboard.

Alpha

You ever done a freeze frame on the video to see if you can read the formulas? They never make any sense. I think we can say for sure that you don't need to understand formulas to make movies.

Beta

Is that why they call a bad movie a formula film?

Alpha

Hiss!

SUMMARY

This chapter has provided a scant minimalist introduction to Knowledge As Design. Any teacher interested in using this strategy should consult David Perkins' description of the approach (Perkins, 1986). But although teachers must be thoroughly familiar with the material they teach, students, on the contrary, should be able to begin discussion of a topic with hardly any knowledge of it. One of the great advantages of Thinkback is that it does not require students to know a great deal. All that is required is that they know enough to maintain a discussion beyond the initial level of trivial or superficial comments. A set of questions such as those provided by Knowledge as Design can support the discussion long enough for students to discover how the knowledge they already have connects with the content under investigation. The beauty of Knowledge as Design is that it provides a structure which remains useful long after these preliminary explorations. No matter how much you know about a topic the four design questions can help you refine your knowledge and reveal questions for further research. Knowledge as Design is a scaffold that never needs to be taken away.

Educational techniques that are consistent with a constructivist model of learning demand questions that can be answered at the most introductory level and yet remain insightful in the most advanced contexts. In classrooms with a diverse collection of learners no two students will be in exactly the same place. Teachers cannot permit students the freedom to explore ideas on their own (or in small groups) unless they can do so confident that every student will derive meaningful learning from such exploration. The beauty of the four design questions is that they provide a wide range of application, allowing every student to explore the topic at an appropriate level. Furthermore, the greater the students' experience with the four design questions the more powerful they become. The power of these questions is that they "break the familiar frame of reference, opening up neglected opportunities for understanding and critical and creative thinking."

CHAPTER SIX

Mastering Memory

This book attempts to demonstrate that Thinkback has a wide range of applications. Chapter 6 ventures into a deeper, more complex, level of mathematical thinking than we have yet explored. In addition, we tackle the sometimes unpopular topic of memorization.

The goals of thinking and memorization are often viewed as being opposed to each other. But this is not the case. Having the facts at your finger tips can be a great help in thinking, and strong thinking skills can be a great aid in memorization. Learning to memorize and learning to understand can, at times, go hand in hand. Here are some examples from *The Complete Problem Solver* (Hayes, 1989).

LEARNING MATHEMATICAL FORMULAS

In *The Complete Problem Solver*, Hayes proposed an approach to learning mathematical formulas that is described in the following section. In this chapter, we consider how the Hayes approach might be developed in the context of Thinkback:

> Suppose that you have an assignment that requires you to learn formulas of the sort typically found in physics or engineering texts. There are a number of procedures you can use to make this task easier and more meaningful. We will describe one which makes use of the multiple coding and context strategies.

Physical Interpretation of Equations

One of the most powerful procedures for learning and understanding equations is the process of physical interpretation. By physical interpretation we mean the process in which people make use of knowledge of a physical situation, perhaps in the form of sketches or visual images, to help them understand or learn an equation.

One way we can use physical interpretation is to help us remember whether a quantity should be placed in the numerator or denominator of an equation.

Before describing how this works, let me mention a property of equations which the math haters in the audience may either have forgotten or never learned in the first place. Consider this arbitrary equation:

$$X = \frac{(A \cdot B) + C}{(D + E)F}$$

How does X change with A, B, C, D, E, and F?

The fact I want you to notice is that

1. X gets *bigger* as A, B, and C get bigger *because those quantities* are in the numerator, and
2. X gets *smaller* as D, E, and F get bigger *because those three quantities* are in the denominator.

Now, suppose that you wanted to remember the equation for the force of gravity between two objects. You know that the force, F, is equal to some combination of G, a constant, M_1 and M_2, the masses of the objects, and r, the distance between them. You think it might be

a. $F = GM_1M_2r^2$ or
b. $F = GM_1M_2/r^2$ or perhaps
c. $F = Gr^2/M_1M_2$

Physical interpretation might involve imagining ourselves floating in space holding two large globes apart. If either of the globes were very heavy, we would expect that it would be harder to hold them apart than if both were light. Since force increases as either of the masses (M's) increases, the masses must be in the numerator. (Why?)

As we push the globes farther apart, the force of attraction between them will decrease as the force of attraction between two magnets decreases as we pull them apart. Since the force decreases as distance, r, increases, r must be in the denominator. (Why?) Of the three equations above, only (b), $F = GM_1M_2/r^2$, satisfies these relations. It is, in fact, the correct equation. (Hayes, 1989, pp. 189–190)

The key idea here is to ask the question "how does X change with A?" But to be able to answer that question, we must know how to separate out the individual relationships within complex interconnected relations. In order to build student skills in this area we start with a much simpler example than Dr. Hayes used.

The next dialogue is a good deal more difficult to follow than those that have preceded it. By now you will have advanced your own skills at interpreting dialogues and at reading the mental *thought images* they contain. Two additional complications have been added to the discourse in this dialogue. The level of mathematical thinking has been raised and the role of the listener has been expanded. The listener in this case continually probes the problem solver's understanding by raising one possible misconception after another. It is not revealed, nor does it matter, whether these misconceptions are really the way the listener sees things or just playful probes that test if the problem solver really understands the material.

ACCELERATING THOUGHT

Problem

Apply the Hayes approach to the equation distance equals rate times time, $d = rt$.

Problem Solver

I find all these letters a bit confusing.
So I am going to consider the case when $r = 6$.

Listener

What does that mean?

Problem Solver

It means that the rate is 6, let's say 6 miles per hour—a slow jog.
Then the equation is $d = 6t$. or distance equals 6 times time.
So as t gets bigger d gets bigger. As time goes by you cover more and more distance.
For example, if t is 3 hours then d is 18 miles.

Listener

The Listener is confused by the conclusion the Problem Solver has reached.

You said d is 18??
Then d is bigger than t? That seems backwards.

The Problem Solver does not understand why the Listener is confused.

Problem Solver

Backwards?
Why backwards?

The Listener is displaying a common algebraic misconception. This misconception stems from reading the equation as though it were a picture rather than a set of instructions for actions to be taken.

Listener

Well look at the equation. It says $d = 6t$. It is clear that t is 6 times bigger than d.

The Problem Solver now attempts to help the Listener.

Problem Solver

Six times bigger? Yes, it does look that way. $d = 6t$
But if I multiply 6 times t (which in this case is 3) I get 18 and the equation then says $d = 18$.
And 18 is 6 times bigger than 3.
So which is it? Is d six times bigger than t or is t six times bigger than d?

Listener

Well, looking at the equation it sure looks like t is bigger.

Problem Solver

Yes, it does. But you can't believe everything you read.

Listener

You mean mathematics is wrong?

Problem Solver

The Problem Solver continues to attempt to help the Listener.

Well no, but maybe our way of looking at it is wrong.
When we write the 6 next to the *t* we make it look like we are making *t* six times bigger.
But that is not what it means. The number *t* will be what ever it is. It doesn't change. So *t* is *t*.
The new number we get, 6 times *t*, is in this case 18 and it is just a number.
The equal sign then tells us that 18 happens to be the value of *d*.

Listener

The Listener understands what the Problem Solver has said but does not feel convinced by it.

It still looks wrong to me, but I see what you are saying. I have a clear thought image even though I don't think I can read it.

Problem Solver

So we agree that *d* gets bigger as *t* gets bigger, we just are not too sure which one is the biggest.

Listener

Yes.

Problem Solver

And *d* also gets bigger as 6 gets bigger.

Listener

Six gets bigger? My thought image has gone completely out of focus.

Problem Solver

Well 6 does not really get bigger, what I mean is the value for *r* which I chose to be 6. This value for *r* could get bigger or smaller. If it gets bigger then *d* gets bigger, bigger than 18, and if it gets smaller then *d* gets smaller than 18.

Listener

Here the Listener displays another kind of algebraic misconception.

What if t isn't 3? Then *r* might get bigger and *d* still would not be as big as 18.

Problem Solver

The Problem Solver does not understand the source of the Listener's confusion.

Like?

Listener

The Listemer attempts to explain the confusion.

Like if *r* is 7 (which is bigger than 6) and *t* is 2. Then *d* is 14 which is smaller than 18. So *r* got bigger and *d* got smaller.

Problem Solver

The Problem Solver understands the Listener's problem.

Yes, but you aren't controlling variables.

Listener

Controlling what? I don't understand. My thought image is shutting down.

Problem Solver

The Problem Solver attempts to explain.

Controlling variables means we can only change one thing at a time. You can't change both rate and time at the same time.

Listener

The Listener tries to defend his view.

Why not? I could be running at 6 miles per hour for 3 hours or if I went faster, like 7 miles per hour, I would get tired and quit after 2 hours. It doesn't make any sense that I would run faster and still run as long a time.

Problem Solver

The Problem Solver explains in more detail.

Yes, that is true.
But if you want to see how one thing depends on another you can only change one thing at a time. If I change rate, I must leave time constant so I can see how changing rate influences distance.

Listener

The Listener further defends his view.

But if I run faster I won't necessarily go further, I might run so fast I get tired very quickly and not go very far at all. So you can't fix one and change the other, it doesn't work that way.

Problem Solver

The Problem Solver tries again.

What you are saying is that the formula $d = rt$ is not a good formula for you. You need a more complicated formula that takes into consideration what happens when you get tired. According to the math formula r might be 100 miles per hour. The formula would let you run at 100 miles per hour. That does not make any sense. We are looking at how the formula works not at how you work. According to the formula if I make t constant and increase r then d will also increase. And if I make r constant and increase t then d will increase.

Listener

The Listener drops the issue and moves on.

So, how does this help us remember the formula?

Problem Solver

Well, first I have to remember that there are three parts: distance, rate, and time. And that there are only three parts, like there is nothing about getting tired.

Listener

Yes.

Problem Solver

And then I can see that distance will increase the longer we go. It will also increase the faster we go.
So I can write $d = rt$.

I know it is not $d = r/t$ or $d = t/r$ because if it were then in the first case d would get smaller as t got bigger and in the second d would get smaller as r got bigger.

Listener

The Listener sees a hole in the Problem Solver's logic.

So why isn't the formula $d = r + t$?
In that case d gets bigger as r gets bigger, and d also gets bigger as t gets bigger.

Problem Solver

Yes, but in the wrong way.
I am not sure I know how to answer your question. I think you just have to remember if it is addition or multiplication. I don't think the method we have here helps you tell which is which.

REVIEW OF PROBLEM SOLUTION

The listener in this dialogue is a truly "expert" novice. No one student is likely to exhibit all of the misconceptions and confusions that this listener brings forth. Furthermore, for any real student, these confusions are much more persistent than suggested by this dialogue. In practice, the explanations given by the problem solver would not have been adequate to convert the listener's thinking. What this dialogue demonstrates is not what would happen in an actual classroom situation, but rather how listener–problem solver dialogues can be written to show teachers what to look out for while they are teaching a particular topic. Many math teachers have never before seen the misconceptions revealed in this dialogue, and yet extensive research has shown that these very misconceptions are found in about 90% of the college population. Without Thinkback, most teachers have had to operate as though blind to the landscape in which they practiced.

The dialogue also reveals another very important aspect of the Thinkback strategy. We do not know whether the listener has misconceptions about mathematics or simply uses them to prod the problem solver. It does not matter. The effect is the same. Thus, a listener who is a complete novice in the area under study may provide feedback to the problem solver that is on par with what the most seasoned expert might provide. Obviously, the novice cannot do everything the expert would do. But an expert armed with 30 powerful assistants can get a great deal more done than one who works alone, rolling, rolling, and rolling the verbal instruction boulder.

RESISTING THOUGHT

Problem

Apply the Hayes method to Ohm's Law: V = IR.

Problem Solver

V = IR looks just like d = rt. But I find it much harder because I am not too sure what V, I, and R mean.
Actually I know V is for volts or voltage and I is for current (why the letter I is used for current is a mystery to me)and R is for resistance.
But in the context of electricity I am not too sure what these things really are.
So if what we did with d = rt still holds true, then as I increases V increases and as R increases V increases.

Listener

The Listener may be confused or just pretending in order to get the Problem Solver to explain in more detail.

How can V increase as R increases? If R is resistance, resistance slows things down. How can more resistance make more of something else, it ought to be less.

Problem Solver

Well, we don't really know what voltage is. If voltage is like frustration, more resistance can create more frustration.
So, if current is the amount of stuff that goes by—maybe the number of cars going by on the road. If there are lots of cars there will be lots of frustration.
And if resistance is, ... like how narrow the road is. It would have to get bigger the narrower the road. So a one-lane road would have a bigger resistance than a three-lane road.

Listener

Again, the Listener may or may not know the answer—the

How is that possible? How can a one-lane road have a bigger number than a 3-lane road?

point here is to make the Problem Solver describe things is more detail.

Problem Solver

Well, I don't know ...
It could be like an inverse. Say, divide the width of the road into 1. Then a 1-lane road gives us 1, a 2-lane road ½, a 3-lane road $^1/_3$ ...

Listener

I guess that works.

Problem Solver

So now I can remember the formula because I know there is more frustration when there is more traffic (more current) and there is more frustration when there are more obstacles (more resistance). So that means V = IR.

Listener

I am not too sure about any of this. How do you feel about it?

Problem Solver

I don't know. I don't think the physics is really right. But image of traffic and such might help me remember the formula.

FAR FLUNG THOUGHT

Problem

Aircraft carriers have steam driven catapults to push planes up to take-off speed. The maximum speed of the plane at the end of the push can be determined from the formula:

$$S^2 = 2FD/M$$

In this formula S is the plane's speed, M is the mass of the plane, F is the force of the catapult and D is the distance the plane is pushed.

Use the Hayes method to remember this formula.

Problem Solver

First, I have to remember that the speed is squared, I don't see any good way to remember that.
Next I have to remember the 2 on the right side, again I have no good way to remember that either.
The more force the faster the plane will go so F should be on top.

Listener

Yes

Problem Solver

The more distance the plane is pushed the faster it will be going, so D should be on top too.

Listener

Why?

Problem Solver

The further you push and the longer you push the more chance there is to pick up speed. But the heavier the plane the less effect the pushing will have and the slower it will be going, so M should be on the bottom.

Listener

Are you sure?
A fast heavy object has more speed ... like it keeps going longer on its own.

Problem Solver

Hmmmmm.
I think that is more momentum that it has that keeps it going. It is not more speed. A big boat can be going very slowly but it is very hard to stop.

Listener

So what do you get?

Problem Solver

From Hayes I get S = FD/M and then I have to use raw memory to add the square and the factor of two to make it.

$$S^2 = 2FD/M$$

Listener

I am not sure I would want to count on that in an exam.

Problem Solver

Me neither.

SUMMARY

Although the Hayes strategy depends on an understanding of what the variables in the equation mean and how they relate to each other, students who do not have this knowledge can still benefit from applying the strategy within the context of Thinkback. They may not generate a fool-prove way to remember the formula, but they are likely to generate a better understanding of some of the concepts involved. Working alone they would be much less likely to make effective headway, and they certainly would not have as good a time. A very important aspect of Thinkback is that it can make learning fun even in situations that students might normally find unpleasant. This is one of the most important benefits of Thinkback. It makes both learning *and teaching* much more effective because it makes them more interesting, exciting and fun.

Hayes (1989) has filled the *Complete Problem Solver* with a vast array of useful thinking, learning, and problem solving strategies, many of which are taken from research in cognitive science. In this chapter, we have been able to glance quickly at only one of these. Readers who enjoy learning about such strategies will find his book to be a fabulous feast.

CHAPTER SEVEN

Mapping Your Mind

CONCEPT MAPS

Knowing what you know is not as simple as it might seem. Major legal cases have been fought over the issue of "what did the defendant know and when did he know it?" Added to these two important questions, a humorist has added "... and did he know that he knew it?"

Consider how often you have said in frustration, "I knew that." The painful fact is that much of what we know remains disconnected from other parts of our knowledge. This means that we often don't recognize that we have knowledge that could be useful to us. We might know that there are 8 ounces in a cup and 16 ounces in a pound and still not be too sure what a cup of water weighs. This might be because we have not yet connected the ounces used with liquid measure and those used in weights. (They only equate exactly when we are measuring water.)

When we say we have a good grasp of a concept what we mean is that we know how the different parts are related. One can say "I understand Jim" but what is really meant is that one sees how the different parts of Jim's feelings and beliefs are connected to each other. Usually, we sense we understand without being able to explicitly make all the connections; we cannot put the sense we have into words or pictures.

Concept mapping is a technique for putting the various connections in a concept into words and pictures. This can be a tremendous help both for recognizing the connections we have already made and for seeing new connections we have not yet discovered. In this chapter, we review the work of Professor Joseph Novak, a leading authority on concept maps and their use in teaching. We will explore how Thinkback can be combined with some of the techniques Dr. Novak employed in *Learning, Creating, and Using Knowledge* (1998).

First let us look at the objectives Dr. Novak seeks to accomplish with concept mapping.

> I will claim that *the central purpose of education is to empower learners to take charge of their own meaning making*. Meaning making involves thinking, feeling, and acting, and all three of these aspects must be integrated for significant new learning, and especially in new knowledge creation. (p. 9)

> When education is most effective, managers become teachers, teachers are also learners, and learners are also teachers. This can be especially true where learners are engaged in cooperative learning activities. (p. 13)

Following these cues, we let the learners teach us how to build a concept map by watching what they do in a Thinkback cooperative learning activity. Rather than describe how a cognitive map works, we will, instead, watch two students encounter one. The students have access to Dr. Novak's book and are trying to understand the diagram below. In this case the problem solver's problem is to read and interpret the diagram.

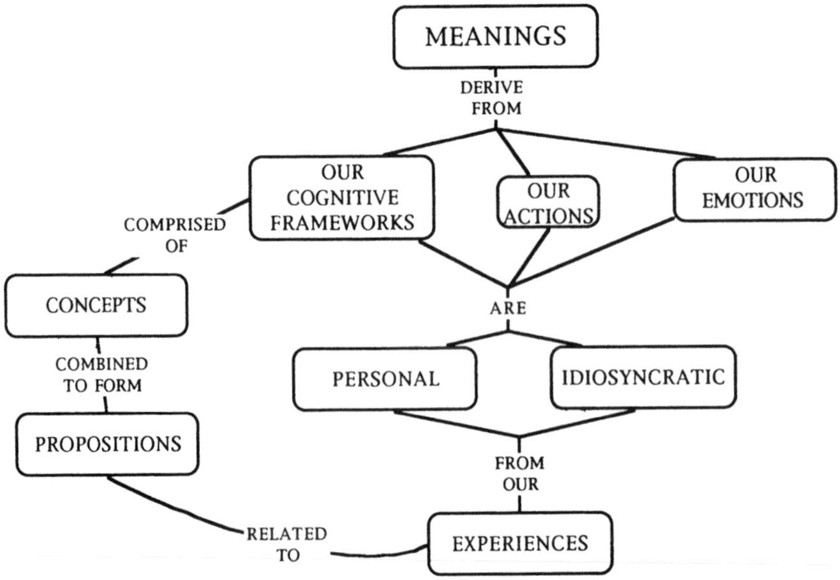

Problem Solver

So this diagram is supposed to tell us what the meaning of meaning is.

Listener

Sounds like a vicious circle to me.

Problem Solver

The Problem Solver has incorporated good listener questioning into his own thinking.

Certainly is vicious. I am not sure about the circle.
Let me start reading the diagram from the top.
At the top I see "meanings."
These are linked to three boxes and the link is labeled "derive from." The three boxes are: "our cognitive frameworks," "our actions," and "our emotions."
So what does this mean to me?

I am not sure what a cognitive framework is.
But I think I see how meaning is derived from our actions. The meaning I am making now of this diagram is very much related to my, or rather our, action of reading this together in a Thinkback mode.

Listener

This is a modest hint but it does not disrupt the Problem Solver

How do you feel about that?

Problem Solver

How do I feel? Right now, rather confused and a little bit silly.
Oh! Were you asking about my emotions, about how my emotions are influencing the meaning of meanings? I guess right now I am a little tense and my emotions are getting in the way of my getting a clear sense of the meaning of this diagram.
Let me see if I can get a better example of how meanings derive from emotions. Take snow. The meaning of snow is for me associated with good feelings from skiing. But for someone who has been stuck in a bad snow storm or an avalanche, perhaps even nearly died in one, that person might have bad feelings about snow. For me snow means something good; for the avalanche victim snow could mean something bad.

Listener

Again, the Listener is slightly directing with this question but also trying to get more detail on how the Problem Solver is thinking.

So what is a cognitive framework?

Problem Solver

Here the Problem Solver is looking back at the diagram to see if it has clues on what is intended by "cognitive framework."

I told you I don't really know. But it seems to have something to do with what you already know. So the meaning of something derives, in part, from what you already know.
Let me see what links "our cognitive frameworks" has and whether that helps me better understand it.

It is "composed of" "concepts." That makes sense. Knowledge is composed of concepts.
The other link says "are" "personal" and "idiosyncratic."
What is the difference?

Listener

What difference?

Problem Solver:

What is the difference between personal and idiosyncratic? Idiosyncratic means unique to the individual. Personal means your own. I don't see much difference, though personal need not be unique.

Listener

I see what you are saying and I can't add anything more myself.

Problem Solver

Then it says "concepts" can be "combined to form" "propositions" and that "propositions" are "related to" "experiences." On the other side it says that "personal" and "idiosyncratic" come "from our" "experiences."

So everything comes from experiences. It takes different paths but it ends up as meanings.

Listener

What paths?

Problem Solver

Well, there are three major paths: cognitive frameworks, actions, and emotions. Experience filtered through these three paths becomes meaning.

Listener

Why three?

Problem Solver

Well, the diagram shows just three but maybe there are more. I am trying to think. There is nothing about the dictionary. When we want to find what a word means we usually look in the dictionary. There is nothing about definitions. It seems to imply that meaning is all based on personal experience and never on learning from others.

Listener

Are you sure there is no place for the dictionary in the current diagram?

Problem Solver

Well, you could say that reading the dictionary is an experience. And, I guess, the "propositions" and concepts that "comprise" "our cognitive frameworks" could come from what we read and are told. But why would the use of dictionaries be hidden in this manner? Why not make such sources of information more obvious?

Listener

The Listener is essentially reflecting back a question the Problem Solver already asked himself.

Any ideas? Why might these ideas have been hidden in that manner?

Problem Solver

Hmmm ...

It could be that the author wanted to emphasize that even though the definition is in the dictionary each of us might read the dictionary a little differently. But I still find that an incomplete picture.

Listener

Why do you say that?

Problem Solver

Well, words don't mean anything unless the meaning is shared by a group of people. If a word has a completely idiosyncratic meaning it is no use as a word. This concept map does not show how meanings get to be shared.

Listener

Or at least we don't see how it shows that. Why don't we switch roles and try another map? My problem will be to read the diagram on page 65.

Problem Solver

Students switch roles.

This looks like some kid's concept of something; I guess it is Denny's concept. It is his concept of water or river. No, it has to be water because of the link "is in a."

Listener

Why do you say that?

Problem Solver

Because if "river" was the concept the link would read "contains."

So "water" has five links. Three are labeled "can be," one is "is in a" and one is not labeled. Basically they are all showing ways water can be.

Listener

Instances of:

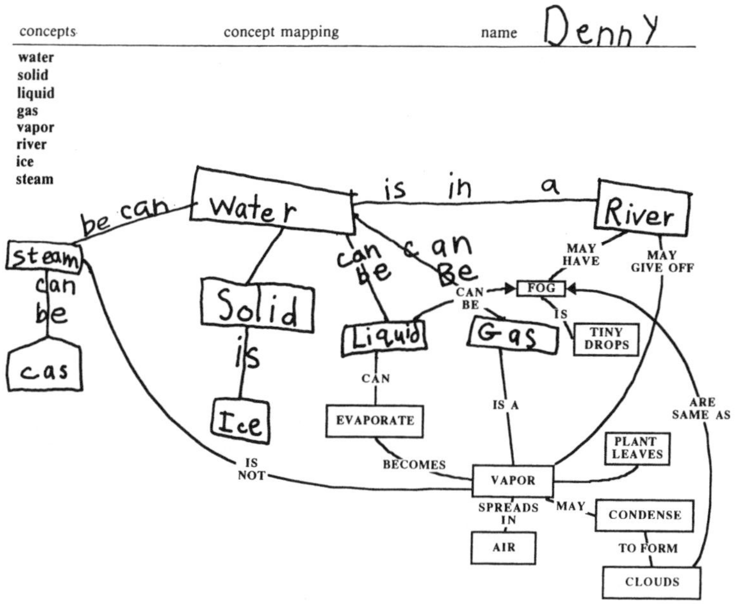

Problem Solver

You mean like back with Perkins' Knowledge As Design. I suppose there ought to be some relationship. Both Concept Mapping and Knowledge As Design attempt to describe our knowledge.
So, according to Denny, water can be: "steam," "solid," "liquid," "gas" or "in a river."
When it is solid it is "ice."
When it is steam it is "cas"—I think he means gas.
When it is liquid it can "evaporate" or be "fog."
When it is gas it is a "vapor."
When it is in a river it may have "fog" or give off "vapor"
There is a certain lack of symmetry here.

Listener

How?

Problem Solver

Well, we have steam and gas as two separate things but we don't see different kinds of liquid or ice. If we are separating fog, steam, vapor and gas then shouldn't we also separate ice, snow, clear ice and cloudy ice?

What is interesting, is we can't tell if Denny has these concepts confused or whether it is just that he isn't very careful in how he draws his concept map. He may be putting down the first thing that pops into his head without asking what else should be thought of that way. He seems to be really into the fog and vapor concepts and not much interested in the liquid and solid phases.

Listener

So his interests determine his map?

Problem Solver

His interests seem to shape what parts of the map he spends time drawing, and this means we have to be careful in how we interpret what he draws. We really ought to be there asking him questions so we can see what parts he could fill out but just hs not bothered to do so.

Listener

You mean sort of like having a listener sitting there with him?

Problem Solver

Yes, a combination of Thinkback and Concept Mapping.

SUMMARY

Concept mapping shows how different concepts are related to each other or, in the case of a single concept, the connections between its various attributes. The map displays different concepts and attributes spread out over a sheet of paper with links drawn between them. Each link is labeled to indicate what kind of connection it represents. The act of drawing or reading a concept map can be highly instructive as it forces one to consider the full array of relationships between different elements. Often these links are connections that we are only dimly aware of in any conscious sense. Bringing the links into conscious awareness broadens our understanding of the concepts involved.

The Thinkback process forces the map designer to explain reasons for deciding to display a link as well as the reasons for deciding that certain other links should not be included. The structure of the concept map is transformed from a static representation frozen in time to a dynamic image of colliding attributes that wax and wane as the map builder restructures the territory. Thus the power of concept mapping is increased to provide insight not just into how our concepts are structured but also into how we continue to adapt concepts as we gain experience in their application.

BUILDING A CONCEPT MAP OF THE THINKBACK STRATEGY

The following exercise demonstrates how the act of drawing a concept map, in conjunction with Thinkback, can help students better know what they know. It also looks back on the concept of Thinkback and maps out that terrain.

	Problem Solver
Student reads the following:	So our problem is to draw a concept map for the Thinkback Strategy. Why don't we start by seeing what Novak has to say about making a map.

How To Build a Concept Map

1. Identify a focus question that addresses the problem, issues, or knowledge domain you wish to map. Guided by this question, identify 10 to 20 concepts that are pertinent to the question and list these. Some people find it helpful to write the concept labels on separate cards or Post-its™ so that they can be moved around. If you work with computer software for mapping, produce a list of concepts on your computer. Concept labels should be a single word, or at most two or three words.
2. Rank order the concepts by placing the broadest and most inclusive idea at the top of the map. It is sometimes difficult to identify the broadest, most inclusive concept. It is helpful to reflect on your focus question to help decide the ranking of the concepts. Sometimes this process leads to modification of the focus question or writing a new focus question.
3. Work down the list and add more concepts as needed.
4. Begin to build your map by placing the most inclusive, most general concept(s) at the top. Usually there will be only one, two, or three most general concepts at the top of the map.
5. Next select the two, three, or four subconcepts to place under each general concept. Avoid placing more than three or four concepts under any other concept. If there seem to be six or eight concepts that belong under a major concept or subconcept, it is usually possible to identify some appropriate concept of intermediate inclusiveness, thus creating another level of hierarchy in your map.

6. Connect the concepts by lines. Label the lines with one or a few linking words. The linking words should define the relationship between the two concepts so that it reads as a valid statement or proposition. The connection creates meaning. When you hierarchically link together a large number of related ideas, you can see the structure of meaning for a given subject domain.
7. Rework the structure of your map, which may include adding, subtracting, or changing superordinate concepts. You may need to do this reworking several times, and in fact this process can go on indefinitely as you gain new knowledge or new insights. This is where Post-its™ are helpful, or better still, computer software for creating maps.
8. Look for crosslinks between concepts in different sections of the map and label these lines. Crosslinks can often help to see new, creative relationships in the knowledge domain.
9. Specific examples of concepts can be attached to the concept labels (e.g., golden retriever is a specific example of a dog breed).
10. Concept maps could be made in many different forms for the same set of concepts. There is no one way to draw a concept map. As your understanding of relationships between concepts changes, so will your maps.

Problem Solver

I am going to start by making a list of key words.

Listener

Key words?

Problem Solver

Well, I will write them down as words but they are really the labels given to concepts, or rather sub concepts, that form the parts of Thinkback. For example: listener, problem solver, problem, talking aloud, or, rather, thinking aloud, listener questions, that sort of thing. Then there is the image of videotape playback, the thought image, the slow motion of moving through step by step.

Listener
Problem Solver
Problem
Talking Aloud—Thinking Aloud
Listener Questions

Thought Image
    Slow motion
    Step by Step

Listener

Where does it start? What is the key concept off of which the others branch out?

Problem Solver

I have not decided that yet. I don't think that is an easy question to answer. There are the roles (of listener and problem solver) then there are *activities* that should be practiced in each role. There is the concept of a mental trace, a mental thought image. There is the self-correcting nature of the entire process that makes the whole more than the sum of its parts. It is difficult to know which of these to pick as most important.

Roles
    Listener
    Problem Solver
Activities
Concept
    Thought Image

Listener

The Listener checks to make sure his image of the Problem Solver's thought is correct.

So right now your view is a bit of a blur, nothing comes sharply into focus?

Problem Solver

No, quite the opposite. I think too many things come sharply into focus. It is all quite vivid. What is missing is an organizing hierarchy. I am not even sure that there should be one. It seems to me that imposing a hierarchy distorts the picture. By making a cognitive map I am going to be artificially changing the way I perceive Thinkback.

Listener

And that does not happen with other maps?

Problem Solver

No, well perhaps yes. I don't think it is as severe but even a road map distorts geography. I see what you are, perhaps, saying.
So, I should charge ahead and make a cognitive map even though it means over simplifying the concept. I can always make another map that stresses some other perspective if I feel my map is too distorted.
OK, here goes.
I am going to take the thought image as the central idea. It is the recording of the mind's work that lets us see what thinking is really like. I can't point to the thought image, it isn't a single thing, but it is the central concept that motivates all else.
Two links off the thought image will both be labeled "made by" and go to: the problem solver and the listener.

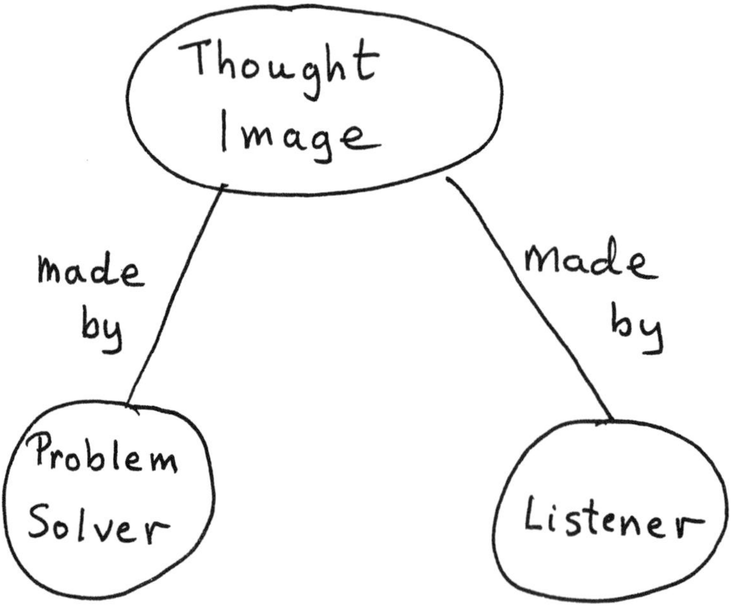

Listener

Why them? What is your thinking behind that.

Problem Solver

Well, they make the thought image. The way they make it is by thinking aloud and active listening. I haven't really yet thought whether I want those boxes to represent roles or actions. Then there is also the problem. Some problems make better thought images than others. Also the learning technique being used is important.
And there is also the teacher.

Listener

The teacher?

Problem Solver

Yes, the teacher is very important. If the teacher doesn't shut up and keep out of the way, you are not going to get a good thought image. Also the teacher can help a great deal by asking the right question at the right time.

Listener

We have seen that?

Problem Solver

Well no, not so far in this book. We have seen no examples of teachers working with a listener/problem solver pair. Maybe we should suggest that for some future book.

Apparently, both the Problem Solver and the Listener were able to read this book as it was being written.

Listener

What is going on with your concept map?

Problem Solver

Good question, Let me try to sketch the big picture and then worry about the details. So I have a thought image made by listener and problem solver. I then have the listener and problem solver looking at the thought image to learn about thinking. They are making corrections all the time. Sometimes these are big strategy changes and sometimes just small details.

Listener

Like?

Problem Solver

Like with the graphic organizers the way Martha noticed that the top row had not been filled and that she needed to, in order to define what the organizer was all about.

Listener

Yeah, and I don't think Alpha and Beta ever got theirs filled in for the order of the numbers. So are these examples of little details or big strategy changes?

Problem Solver

That depends. In these cases I think they were more in the way of minor changes. Alpha and Beta did fine without catching their mistake. But for some people learning to be more systematic and careful might be a major strategy change.

Listener

So do we have an example of a major strategy change?

Problem Solver

Well, when Alpha figured out that it was not enough just to see which decimal had the most number of places to the right, if that insight stuck, I would consider that a major strategy change.
But getting back to the concept map, I am not too sure how to represent any of this information on the map.
I guess I want some new links between the problem solver, the listener and the thought image. These would be labeled observes.

These multiple links are confusing. I am going to change my mind. I am going to use actions not roles. I am going to have to make an entirely new map.
So we have the thought image. It is "made by" "thinking aloud" and "active listening." It is also "observed by" "reflective thinkers." No, that is a role. It is observed by "reflective thinking." Reflective thinking needs to be linked somehow to changing thought patterns.

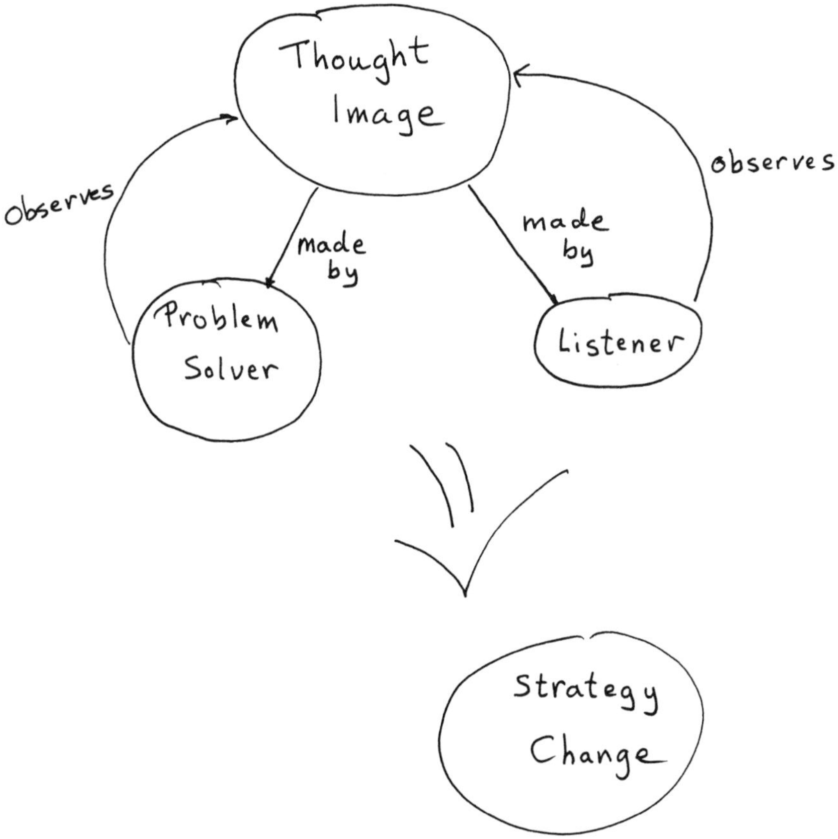

Listener

Just thought patterns? How about concepts?

Problem Solver

Well, a concept might be considered a thought pattern. But, I take your point. I will add concepts next to thought patterns.

Listener

Why are you quiet, what are you thinking?

Problem Solver

I am trying to look at the big picture. I want to know what important elements are missing. There is the way that in Thinkback we

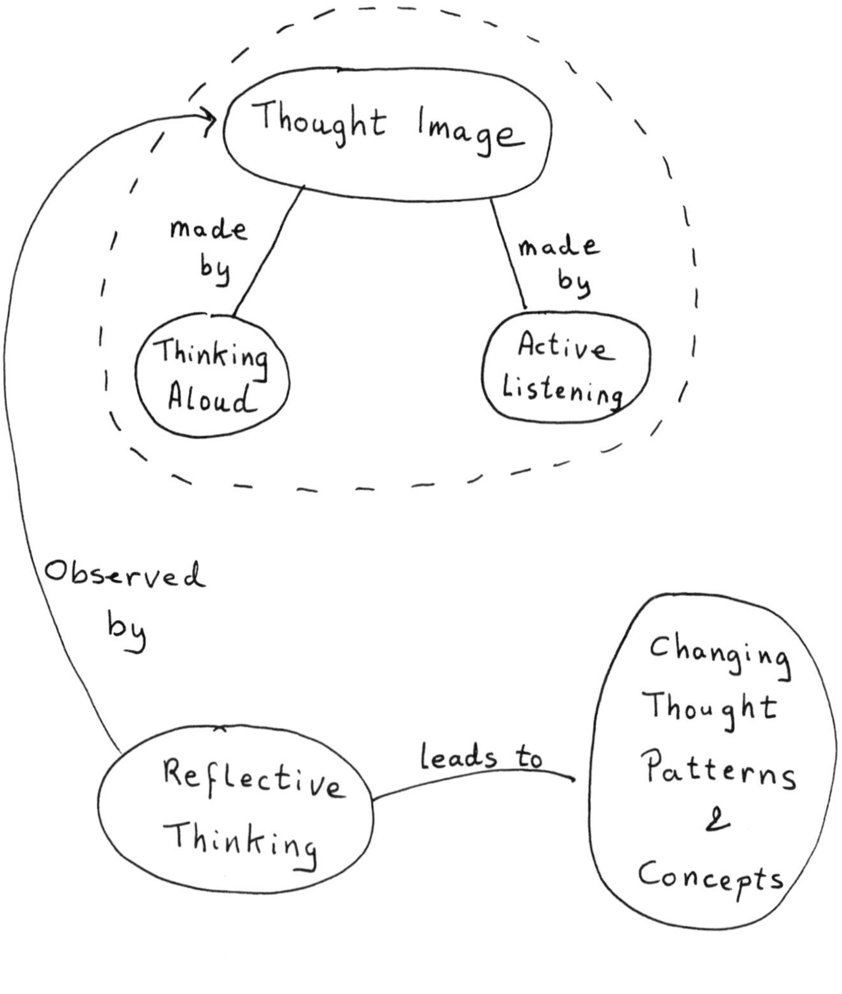

learn so much on our own, without direct input from teachers, textbooks or any form of authority. How does that happen? How can I describe that? Then there is the way things get so much more interesting than they at first seem, and the way time flies by so fast. It changes your whole outlook on learning.

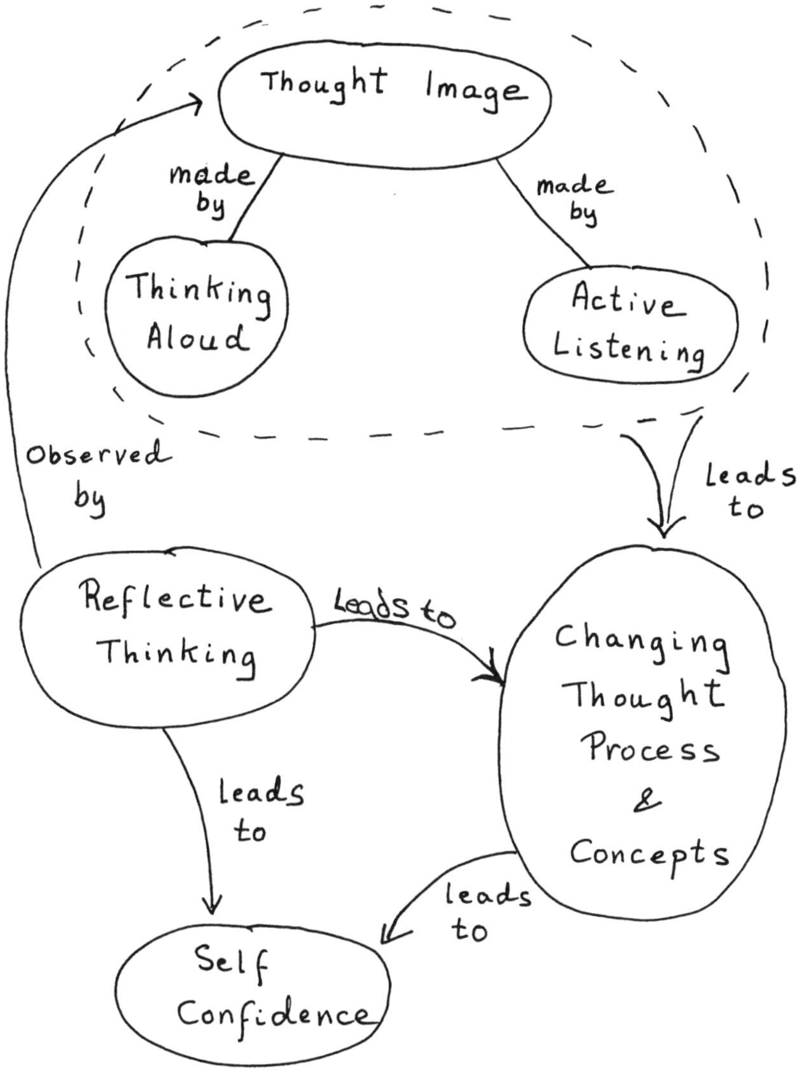

Listener

Isn't that already in the map where you show "reflective thinking" changing "concepts" and "thought patterns"?
What is different about what you are saying?

Problem Solver

Yes, those links show how it happens, I guess. But they don't convey the power or excitement.

Listener

And does a road map show you the scenery?

Problem Solver

No, not unless it has pictures off to the side. Perhaps I need to use that technique. No, there is a better way. I am going to add "self confidence." The whole loop of "reflective thinking" leading to "changed though processes" expressed in "thinking aloud" is itself connected to "self confidence." You learn you can do it yourself. What was it that Novak said: "the central purpose of education is to empower learners to take charge of their own meaning making" (p. 9). That is what Thinkback is really about.

Listener

Maybe, but what happens when the teacher looks at the thought image?
I think that might be pretty important too.

Problem Solver

You mean the teacher can see how we are really thinking and better understand how to help us. You know that makes me think of something else that is important. It is the learning of how to think about thinking. Learning how to read a thought image to stick with the language we are using here. The more you use the process the better you get at it. I suspect that is true for teachers as well as students. I can now listen to my own thoughts much better than I used to and I can listen to yours as well.

Listener

Though often you may not like what you hear.

The Reader's Concept Map of Thinkback

Problem Solver

With my thoughts or your thoughts? No, but seriously, it is so much more interesting and understandable to be able to follow how and why people are saying the things they are saying. Even when it is gibberish; which it usually isn't once you understand the method in the madness.But something is gnawing at me....
Our map is mostly actions but the thought image is a thing. I think the thought image should be a link to "thought process." The critical idea is looking at thought processes and the thought image is a tool you use to do that.

Listener

Are you about to completely remake the map again? Why don't we instead leave that for the reader to do?

Problem Solver

Good idea!
Fitting in the role to the teacher might make this much more complicated. I would be very happy to have someone else do that bit.

SUMMARY

As the end of the previous dialogue suggests, the most useful concept map is the one you make yourself. Don't allow the fledgling effort of two struggling students to substitute for the map you might make on your own. Furthermore don't let this very brief introduction substitute for the thorough presentation provided in *Learning, Creating, and Using Knowledge*. Thinkback is a tool for learning, not a substitute. Comprehensive learning requires reading, writing, mapping, and many other activities as well.

CHAPTER EIGHT

Thinking at Home

This chapter is intended to illustrate how Thinkback might be employed at home. It concerns a conversation at the kitchen table. Mom (M) is taking a course in Instructional Design and needs to practice the application of Professor Lev Landa's Landamatics. She knows she is not going to get the necessary cooperation from her own kids so she has bribed the kid (K) next door with the promise of freshly baked chocolate chip cookies laced with ribbons of marshmallow and a deniable[1] scattering of coarsely crumbled cashews.

The aspect of Landamatics that Mom has to practice is described in the following quote from Reigeluth (1999):

> *Instructional objective 4*: Get students to discover and consciously realize the system of mental operations (Ma) involved in the application of the learned concept, and its definition, to the task of identifying objects belonging or not belonging to the defined class.... *Instructional objective 5*: Get students to explicitly formulate the corresponding system of instructions (Mp). (p. 351)

The exact meaning of these two instructional objectives is clarified in the following discussion. However, the dialogue does not explain Landamatics or the full contribution these two instructional objectives make to the total system. For a proper introduction to Landamatics, see Landa (1999). Instructional objectives 4 and 5 carry very high demands for reflective thinking. They are, therefore, most easily mastered by students who are already very skilled in Thinkback. Fortunately the kid from next door has had plenty of practice.

M

Tell me what you learned in school today.

K

Bars, we learned about bars.

M

Bears? You learned about bears in biology?

K

No, bars, like those long thin things.

M

No, what kind of bars are you talking about? I don't think they teach that in school.

K

Like in math class, you have this chart or graph and it has got bars on it.

M

Oh! Those kind of bars. Tell me about them. How do they work?

K

When will the cookies be ready?

M

They are baking. They smell good, don't they? Maybe another few minutes. But tell me about the bars.

K

Well, like the long ones mean more.

M

More?

K

More stuff. More of whatever it is you are charting. We charted how many uncles and aunts we each had. Suzie had the most so she had the longest bar.
Borrringgg!!!!!

M

Hmmm.
Maybe you can help me understand this. I got a book last week. It is called *The Consumer's Guide to Effective Environmental Choices* (Brower & Leon, 1999). It has all sort of graphs in it. Here is one on page 65.

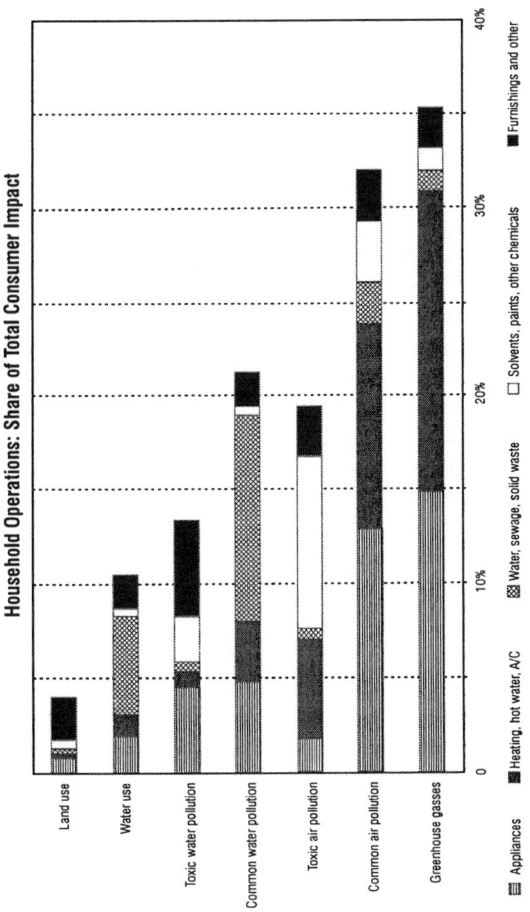

From *The Consumer's Guide to Effective Environmental Choices* by Brower and Leon (1999). Copyright © 1999 by The Union of Concerned Scientists. Reprinted by permission of Three Rivers Press, a division of Random House, Inc.

K

Wow, this is nothing like school. It is very confusing. But I guess Greenhouse gases wins.

M

Wins?

K

Well the height of the bars tells you which one has the most and the tallest bar is Greenhouse with Common air pollution a close second.

M

But what does that mean?

K

Mean? I gotta tell you what this means?
Maybe I had better read what it says next to the chart.
On the top it says "Household Operations: Share of Total Consumer Impact"—I am not too sure just now what that means.
Then on the side it lists several things: "Land use, Water use, Toxic water pollution"—These all seem to be bad things—"Common water pollution, Toxic air pollution, Common air pollution, Greenhouse gases."
Then at the bottom of the page there are these little boxes labeled "Appliances; Heating, hot water, AC; Water, sewage, solid waste; Solvents, paints, other chemicals, Furnishings and other."

M

So what is it all about?

K

What about the cookies?

M

Yes, you are right they should be ready. I will take them out of the oven. But they will need time to cool.

K

I think it is sort of like the map program I have on my computer.

M

The map program?

K

Yes, it has this color key that shows you green means forest and yellow means grass lands, brown is bare ground ... that sort of thing.
Well, here the first box means appliances like the oven, the refrigerator, the stove. The second box means heating, hot water and air conditioning.

M

Here, I think this one is ready. (Mom hands the kid a cookie.)

K

(Kid makes stuffing crunching noises ending in sucking sounds associated with teeth welded together by marshmallow.)

M

I think you may understand these graphs better than you let on.

K

These are not so boring.
So, let us look at just the Greenhouse gases. That bar goes all the way up to 35%. Thirty-five percent of what?
The heading says share of consumer impact. So I guess this means that Greenhouse gases are 35% of the consumer impact. Common air pollution is about 32%, Toxic air pollution is nearly 20% and Common water pollution.... Wait, there is a problem!

M

Problem?

K

Yes, this is going to add up to more than 100%.

M

Why is that a problem?

K

Because the sum of all the shares of consumer impact can't be more than 100%. That would mean you have more impact than impact. It is like eating more cookies than there are cookies to eat.

M

Here, have another.

K

(Mumbling between bites) What else is in this book?
Here on page 54 another bar graph "Transportation: Share of Consumer Impact" and over here on page 60, "Food: Share of Consumer Impact."
I think I got it now.
Household Operations contribute 35% of the Greenhouse gases created by consumers. The other 65% come from transportation and from food and that sort of thing.
Also most of the greenhouse gases come from appliances and from heating. Water, solvents and furnishings contribute only a little.

M

How do you know that?

K

Length of bar.
The dark shaded bit goes almost up to 15% and the light shaded bit then goes up to just over 30%. The rest all of it together is less than 5%.

M

So what pollutes more, Appliances or Heat?

K

Well, Appliances go from 0 to nearly 15%, but Heating etc. go from just under 15% to a bit over 30%. So Heating, etc. must account for more than 15% and be a bit bigger than Appliances.

M

So, can you tell me the steps you have to take to determine how much a section of the bar contributes? Say, for example, solvents.

K

Not without another cookie.

M

Just as long as you don't let your mother find out I let you have three.

K

(More sucking sounds after some crunching and mumbling.)

M

What are you thinking?

K

That a fourth cookie would be just right.
It looks like about 2% but I don't have any way to tell that directly. I guess if I took a ruler and measured how long the white bit was I could then measure that same distance along the bottom line starting from 0. That would tell me what percentage the Solvents contribute.

M

How does that work? Can you tell me more precisely?

K

Hmmm. This is not so easy and might require more chocolate.
First, I measure the distance from 0 to 10%. Then I divide that distance by 10. That answer gives me the distance for 1%.
Now I measure the length of the white part of the bar. Next I divide that distance by the distance equal to 1%. The answer gives me the number of 1% units in the white section.

M

So, can you review for me how you tell what a bar graph means?

K

Why? What is this all about anyway?

M

Well, actually it is my homework. I am taking a course on teaching I have to show I can use a teaching strategy....

K

... that makes the student define each step in figuring something. I should have known there was a catch. I always knew there was no such thing as a free cookie.
OK, so a bar graph has these bars.

The length of each bar tells you how much there is of that thing. But you have to read the length off the scale on the side, bottom or where ever. In our case, the scale was in percent of total consumer impact. Sometimes the bar is broken into sections that can be color coded and the like. Then each section of the bar tells you about the amount of each kind of thing. Like in this case we had appliances and heating and such. When you get sections it can be difficult to tell how long each section is. So then you can measure the length of the section with a ruler and compare that length with the markings on the scale.

M

Tell me in steps.

K

In steps? At one cookie per step?

M

Only if you take them home and don't eat them now.

K

Deal.
Step 1: Read graph title to tell what it is about.
Step 2: Find and read the scale to tell how things are measured.
Step 3: Measure the length of the bar or of the section of the bar that you want to know about.
Step 4: Measure the length of the scale from 0 to 10 or to what ever other number is marked on the scale.
Step 5: Divide the length you measured by the number on the scale, 10 or whatever. This will give the length of one unit.
Step 6: Divide the length you got in step 3 by the length of one unit as determined in step 5. This will give the number of units represented by the section of the bar.
Step 7: Collect seven cookies.

M

So what would happen if I got rid of all my appliances?

K

You would not be able to bake cookies, and I would not be able to show you how to read a bar graph.

M

No, what would it mean in terms of greenhouse gases?

K

You would remove 15% of the gases you make as a consumer. You would still be making 85% of what you were before and you would have no cookies to give away.

M

What I really want to know is whether I should buy a new refrigerator.

K

Well, this graph isn't going to tell you that.
I gotta go, bye.

SUMMARY

The previous dialogue demonstrates two aspects of Thinkback. First, how it can be used in an informal, home situation and second, how it can assist in the Landamatics strategy of explicitly defining the steps involved in defining and learning to apply a concept or skill. Landamatics is but one examplar of many specific approaches designed to explicitly break out the components of a complex activity. Thinkback can be usefully applied to any and all of them.

This brief encounter can give only a vague hint of the power and effectiveness of Landamatics. The key feature that makes Landamatics powerful is its ability to make *explicit* the steps and details that normally remain hidden. In this respect it is similar to Thinkback. But Landamatics goes much further. Some Landamatics lessons are based on extensive cognitive research into how people define and use specific concepts. In those lessons Landamatics exposes steps and details that remain hidden under the thinking aloud strategy. For more details see Landa (1974).

In order to better understand the informal application of Thinkback we now return to the kitchen. It is several days later.

K

Thanks for lending me that copy of The Consumer's Guide. It is full all sorts of neat things. I think I can now tell you if you should get a new refridgerator.

M

Really!!

K

It says on page 162 that by 2001 all refrigerators will need to meed a new standard and use 30% less energy than is normal now. So we can try to calculate how much money you will save if you buy one of those new refrigerators.

M

I have to wait until 2001?

K

Maybe not, some dealers may have machines that meet the standard now. If not, they soon will.
So now we have to look at the table on page 68.
Which of these applicances do you have and how many?

M

We have one refrigerator, and of course we have lighting. We have two TVs and use both. We have one dryer, one freezer, a gas oven, a microwave, a dishwasher, a washing machine and five computers. We have no waterbed or swimming pool.

K

Do yoy have electric heat or an electric hot water heater?

M

No.

Electricity Use by Household Lighting and Appliances*

	Average Electricity Use per Unit (kWh/yr)	Average Number of Units per Household	Average Electricity Use per Household (kWh/yr)
Refrigerator	1,155	1.20	1,383
Lighting	940	NA	940
Television	360	2.05	739
Electric dryer	875	0.57	495
Stand-alone freezer	1,240	0.35	429
Range/oven	458	0.60	276
Microwave	191	0.84	161
Waterbed heater	960	0.15	145
Dishwasher	299	0.45	135
Swimming pool pump	2,022	0.05	96
Electric washer	99	0.77	76
Computers	77	0.23	18

*Electricity use is per appliance unit, except lighting, which is per household.

From *The Consumer's Guide to Effective Environmental Choices* by Brower and Leon (1999).

K

Good. OK, so now I can go down the list in the table nad add up all the kilowatt-hours per year (KWh/yr).
That is: 1,155 plus 940 plus 360, plus 360 again for the second TV, plus 875, plus 1,240, plus 0 for the oven as it is gas, plus 191, plus 299, plus 99, plus 5 times 77.

M

Well, actually we only use three of the computers much. The other two are too old.

K

OK, that is 3 times 77. I put it in my calculator and get 5750.

M

So, what does that mean?

K

It means that you are susing about 5,750 kilowatt hours per year. And that your refrigerator is burning up 1,155 of those, about 29%.

M

How do you know that?

K

Well, if you use 5,750 in total, then we get the fraction for the refrigerator by dividing its part (1,150) by the total (5,750). If I plug those into my calculator I get 1,150 divided by 5,750 is 0.2 and that converts to 20%.

M

OK, but so what? That does not tell me if I should buy a new one.

K

You got any more of those cookies hidden away somewhere?

M

Don't tell me you ate the others already!

K

Look, all we have figured out so far is what fraction of your electric bill is caused by that big, old refrigerator. The next step requires you to tell me what your electric bill is—like what was it last month?

M

You are getting awfully nosy.

K

I can't tell you what that old clunker is costing you if you don't give me some information.

M

Well OK, here is where I keep last month's bills. And here is the electric bill. It was $62.13.

K

I am going to call it $60. That makes it easier.
20% of $60 is $12. And $12 times 12 months is $144 per year.

M

So if I spend $800 on a new refrigerator I get to save $144. That does not sound like much of a deal to me.

K

No, I am afraid it is not that simple. We still have a lot of work to do.

M

I think I see why you asked about those cookies.

K

First, a new refrigerator is not going to run for free. It is going to use 30% less. Thirty percent of $144 is $43.20. So all you are going to save each year is $43.

M

That is not very much.

K

It depends, you save it every year. So, after 10 years you have saved $430.
Also you create less pollution. Remember the Greenhouse gases? We saw that 15% of them came from appliances and 20% of the appliance effect is due to the refrigerator.

M

How did you get that?

K

Well, the 15% came from the chart we worked on last time.The 20% came from the calculation we just did.

M

But that was the electric bill not the pollution.

K

It is the same thing. The pollution comes from how much electricity you use. The electric bill also comes from how much you use. So 20% of 15% is just 3%. But we are not done.
The new refrigerator will only reduce electricity use by 30%. So 30% of 3% is just 1%. All you have done is reduce your greenhouse gases by 1%.

M

And save $43.

K

But remember this is for the life of the refrigerator. That is 1% less greenhouse gas every year, 20% in 20 years. And it is $43 off the electric bill every year, $860 in 20 years.

M

So, have they taught you any way to think about things like this in school? I mean spending $800 now to save $860 spread over 20 years.

K

Not while I was listening.

M

I expect they didn't, it might be too useful.
I remember something from an economics course I took in college called "present value" but I don't remember exactly what it was. The idea was something like this. If I have a promise to get money in future years, it has some value right now that is less than the total of what I will get. The reason it is less is I could invest the money and receive interest on it if I had the money right now.

K

Interest? Like the 6% I get on the savings bond Grandma gave me. So how much money do I need to have to get $43 in interest every year? If I get paid 6% interest I need $717 to get $43 every year.

$$[717 \times 0.06 = 43]$$

M

Yes, but at the end of your investment you still have $717 even if you spent all the interest buying cookies. At the end of my refrigerator I have a clunker and no one will take it to the dump for me unless I pay some outrageous sum.

K

So the present value of a $43 yearly saving is less than $717; but we don't know how much less.

M

And we don't know what is the value of cutting my greenhouse gases by 1%?

K

Yeah, this stuff is complicated. They teach you this in economics?

M

Economics, business, something like that, I am not too sure. But what we have already done is a big help. It shows me that a new refrigerator will cost me less than what I actually have to pay for it.

How much less depends on how I think about it. If for simplicity I use a little less than half the $717 the value might be as much as $350, it could be $450 if I think reducing Greenhouse gases is worth $100 to me.

K

So you can think of a $800 refrigerator actually costing more like $350.

	M
	I believe it is time I started looking for one of those 2001 models.

Note: The numbers in this dialogue assume a 10- to 15-year-old refrigerator. If yours is more than 20 years old you will need to rework the calculation or, more simply, run to your nearest appliance dealer.

SUMMARY

Where is the Thinkback in this dialogue? Was the discussion anything more than a casual conversation about refrigerators? Who had the role of the listener and who was the problem solver?

The more acquainted with Thinkback one becomes, the less one needs to use it. The separation between the roles becomes blurred. Persistent questioning about every aspect of the thought process can be limited to those times when such detail is really needed. Conversations can become more natural and free flowing. But the Thinkback-based conversation is built on a solid foundation where deeper understanding can be demanded or provided whenever it is desired.

This kind of fluent use of Thinkback within natural conversation is only possible after the listener's questioning role and the problem solver's thinking aloud have been so thoroughly practiced that they become automatic. Usually this requires many months of practice in which the demands of the separate roles are strictly adhered to. Thinkback is a partial scaffold[2] for thinking. A scaffold is a complex device that is painstakingly constructed only to be torn down again some time after it has been completed. Yet without scaffolds, most of the world's great buildings would still be nothing more than piles of stone.

It is now time to start your own building.

---

[2]Here, it is important to remember that much depends on what the meaning of *is* is taken to be. The scaffolding metaphor *is* only one way of thinking about Thinkback and it is a perspective that some people find misleading. Other perspectives are just as suitable and which perspectives you choose to use are a matter of personal taste.

References

Beyer, B. K. (1997). *Improving student thinking*. Needham Heights, MA: Allyn & Bacon.

Bloom, B. S., & Broder, L. J. (1950). *Problem solving processes of college students*. Chicago: University of Chicago Press.

Brower, M., & Leon, W. (1999). *The consumer's guide to effective environmental choices*. New York: Three Rivers.

Cose, E. (1997). *Color blind: Seeing beyond race in a race-obsessed world*. New York: Harper Collins.

Hayes, J. R. (1989). *The complete problem solver*. Hillsdale, NJ: Lawrence Erlbaum Associates.

Linden, M. J., & Whimbey, A. (1990a). *Analytical writing and thinking*. Hillsdale NJ: Lawrence Erlbaum Associates.

Linden, M. J., & Whimbey, A. (1990b). *Why Johnny can't write*. Hillsdale, NJ: Lawrence Erlbaum Associates.

Novak, J. (1998). *Learning, creating, and using knowledge*. Mahwah, NJ: Lawrence Erlbaum Associates.

Perkins, D. N. (1986). *Knowledge as design*. Hillsdale, NJ: Lawrence Erlbaum Associates.

Reigeluth, C. M. (1999). *Instructional-design theories and models*. Mahwah, NJ: Lawrence Erlbaum Associates.

Whimbey, A., & Blanton, E. L. (1995). *The Whimbey writing program: How to analyze, organize, and write effectively*. Mahwah, NJ: LEArning Inc.

Whimbey, A., Johnson, M. H., Williams, E., Sr., & Linden, M. J. (1993a). *Keys to quick writing skills*. Birmingham, AListener: EBSCO.

Whimbey, A., Johnson, M. H., Williams, E., Sr., & Linden, M. J. (1993b). *Blueprint for educational change*. Atlanta, GA: The Right Combination.

Whimbey, A., & Lochhead, J. (1981). *Developing mathematical skills*. New York, NY: McGraw-Hill.

Whimbey, A. (1989). *Analytical reading and reasoning*. Cary, NC: Innovative Sciences.

Whimbey, A. (1995). *Mastering reading through reasoning*. Cary, NC: Innovative Sciences.

Wiggins, G., & McTighe, J. (1998). *Understanding by design*. Arlington, VA: ASCD.

Author Index

Subject Index